Beyond Spring

Translations from the Asian Classics

月落江天罷釣魚倚柳坐
睡夢華胥營營何必扁舟
契波濛風吹任飄如
辛卯秋泐竜

Beyond Spring

T'ZU

POEMS

OF THE

SUNG

DYNASTY

TRANSLATED BY

Julie Landau

Columbia University Press · New York

*The publisher gratefully acknowledges support toward
the publication given by the Chiang Ching-Kuo
Foundation for International Scholarly
Exchange (USA).*

Grateful acknowledgment is made to the editors and publishers of various periodicals
where some of the translations in this book first appeared: *Asia, The College, The Denver
Quarterly, Encounter, Mss., Renditions,* and *Translation.* Nine tz'u of Chou P'ang-yen first
appeared in *Renditions,* nos. 11 and 12, and in the anthology *Song Without Music*
(Hong Kong: Chinese University Press, 1980).

Columbia University Press
New York   Chichester, West Sussex

Library of Congress Cataloging-in-Publication Data

Landau, Julie.
Beyond spring: tz'u poems of the Sung dynasty / translated by Julie Landau.
p.   cm. —(*Translations from the Asian classics*)
Includes bibliographical references and index.
ISBN 0-231-09678-X
1. Tz'u—Translations into English.   2. Chinese poetry—Sung dynasty,
960–1279.   I. Title.   II. Series.
PL2658.E3L335   1994
895.1'14208—dc20   93-46479
                                                                    CIP

Contents

Illustrations

Acknowledgments

My great good fortune has been that three scholars of such broad scope, with deep understanding of the tradition of which these poems form an integral part, took the time to read and comment on the manuscript. My special thanks go to Professor Hans H. Frankel of Yale for his corrections, his advice on the manuscript, and his support and encouragement toward its publication; to Professor Irving Y. Lo of Indiana University for his careful annotation of the translations—a great help in improving many of them—and his continuing interest; and particularly to Professor Burton Watson of Columbia for guidance and suggestions on all aspects. All three have helped to make this a better book; the shortcomings that remain are entirely my own.

I am grateful to the members of the East Coast Chinese Poetry Group, who, over many years, shared a variety of insights into other Chinese poems that have proved valuable in trying to understand these. Of particular interest to me were the ideas of Yu-kung Kao, Hans Frankel, Stephen Owen, Adele Rickett, Kang-i Sun Chang, Hai-tao T'ang, and Pauline Yu.

I am indebted to Bonnie Crown, the Asia Society, and the New York State Council on the Arts for grants early on, to my friend Long Tang for many hours spent arguing doubtful meanings, to the many editors who have published my translations in literary magazines and pressed me to make a book, and to the staff of the East Asian Library at Columbia, particularly Ken Harlin, who has made everything I ever wanted to do there easy and pleasant.

For their help, their example, and the endless inspiring distractions they provide, I thank my patrons—Henry, Jenny, Zeph, F. A., Hayce, et al.—without them, nothing worthwhile would happen, nor would it be so much fun.

Titles and Abbreviations

Titles

The transliterated tz'u title names the tune to which the poem is written.

Principal texts

NTECT   Wang Chung-wen, ed. *Nan T'ang erh chu tz'u.*
CST   T'ang Kuei-chang, ed. *Ch'üan Sung tz'u.*

*   Starred references indicate that an alternate text was used
for the translation.

Beyond Spring

Introduction

The lineage of *tz'u* is both obscure and shady; its character, wild, exotic, frivolous. First written by prostitutes and performed in the singing houses, tz'u poetry became the favorite of emperors and high ministers. In the Sung dynasty (960–1279) it developed into the prime lyric form in Chinese, a vibrant new element in a very ancient tradition. Tz'u acquired literary refinement far more easily than it could shed its past, and so eluded being taken altogether seriously for centuries. But not even this patina of the disreputable could protect it forever from rules and codification.

The translations in this volume represent the golden age of tz'u, the tenth, eleventh, and twelfth centuries, when it still retained the vernacular freshness of its folk origins and was seriously taken up by the talented literati, people who by inclination and education wrote poetry all the time. Hundreds of thousands of poems by close to four thousand known authors survive from the period.

Sung dynasty China nearly burst at the seams with intellectual energy and artistic achievement. Private academies flourished. Dictionaries, histories, anthologies, and encyclopedias were compiled, documents preserved, antiquities studied, annotated bibliographies made of libraries. There were advances in science and technology, new and better crops, printed books. It is the great age of neo-Confucian philosophy, landscape painting, pottery, calligraphy, prose style, and tz'u poetry.

Creative intensity notwithstanding, Sung China was not strong, not large, and not expansionist: militarily, a disaster. Plagued by wars and border incursions, humiliated by treaties and tribute, kept close to bankruptcy as a result of the combination, the country was lost piecemeal to the "barbarians." In 1127 north China fell to the Chin. The emperor, Hui-tsung (Chao Chi), was captured. The court moved south under a new emperor. No great efforts were made to reclaim the north or Hui-tsung. Southern Sung (1127–1279) was smaller, equally prosperous, and at least as brilliant as the empire had been when it was bigger. It continued to dazzle another century and a half, then fell, to one of its own inventions, gunpowder, successfully used against the Chinese by the Mongols.

Despite these problems and their unfortunate outcome, schools were built; orphanages, old age homes, and hospitals organized. There were fairs, markets, restaurants, street cleaning, street lighting, night life, ships to export silk and porcelain as far as Japan and Egypt. Ideas were utopian and paternalistic, with the Confucian stress on moral responsibility, education, and ability above family connections and wealth. It was an empire administered almost entirely by nonaristocratic civil servants—these were the poets.

Entry into government was by examination. By Sung times, patronage and nepotism had been discredited as an alternative. The exam centered on the Confucian classics and emphasized literary ability, particularly poetry. Anyone who could afford the years of study was eligible. A candidate would have known by heart thousands of poems and been able to express himself with ease in all classical forms. The ideal of the scholar was as *gentleman*, a man of the highest ethical standards and great refinement. That highly literate men, trained in poetry, held sway in the political arena was not only traditional, it was institutionalized through the examination system, a practice already ancient in the tenth century.

Put more romantically, China was for thousands of years governed, on the administrative level, by poets. In the Sung, ideally, though not always in fact, the general welfare was the objective; the means, hotly disputed. Every official was ardently for—or against—something. There was a chaos of reform, counterreform, antireform: social, economic, land, and tax reform, reform in the examination system, in interpretation of the classics, in prose style. What is interesting about the Sung official is that what mattered to him almost as much as his Confucian dedication to the good of the people was his own cultivation. He sought with equal intensity the public good and the private voice.

Although self-expression for the Sung gentleman began with poetry, it did not end there. He painted, did calligraphy, played a musical instrument, designed a garden, collected, compiled, invented. In painting, the scholar completely displaced the academician. There was a shift in value from the realistic representation of nature espoused by the academy to a lyrical one of essence beyond the images favored by the scholar. In calligraphy, too, refinement no longer mattered, what counted was vigor and spontaneity. Style, for the first time, became individual.

To express or evoke in the visual arts, the Sung gentleman might apply ink with strips of paper, elm pods, or rushes. The same sort of impulse in poetry led him to take up a song form from the singing house, erotic in content, disreputable in origin, and mould it into a highly refined and versatile lyric.

Most poetry begins as song: words set to music. In tz'u, the music comes first and the words are "filled in." For the most part, it was the same roughly eight hundred tunes that were filled in again and again.

The music, mostly music of the steppe—to the Chinese, exotic,

3

.

"barbarian" music—had, with some instruments, come to China from Central Asia in the course of the sixth through the eighth centuries. It became popular first in the singing houses; from there, through the back door, with the singing girls who wrote most of the lyrics to these tunes, it arrived at court. It seems to have excited the interest of T'ang emperor Hsüan-tsung (r. 713–755). Musicians and singers of the music school established by the emperor added the new music to their classical training.

Among the earliest extant signed tz'u is one by Hsüan-tsung himself and one attributed to his concubine, Yang Kuei-fei.

Hao shih kuang
The Radiance of Spring

Her hair, as luck would have it, stylish enough for the palace
Her lotus face so fresh
Her body young and fragrant—
No need for Chang Ch'ang to pencil her brows
Heaven made them long

Dear lady, don't think earth shattering beauty lasts
Find a husband
Take this young gallant
And love before the years pile up
Don't waste the radiance of spring!

HSÜAN-TSUNG

4
·

A na ch'ü

Written to give the expert dancer Chang Yün-yung

Moving silk sleeves scattering an endless fragrance
Graceful as red lotus swaying in the autumn mist
A light cloud beneath the peaks that troubles the wind
A willow by the pool, caressing water

ATTRIBUTED TO YANG KUEI-FEI

Signed tz'u from this period, High T'ang, are rare. There were indeed songs written by the poets, and though not acknowledged for posterity (much scholarship has been spent on questions of attribution), they circulated none the less among the courtesans and singing girls.

Rebellion shattered Hsüan-tsung's reign and scattered the musicians and singers of the palace school into entertainment quarters of several major cities. The songs, already a popular genre, gained status through their connection to the court.

In the tenth century the first tz'u anthology by known authors, minor civil servants writing between mid-ninth and mid-tenth centuries in Szechuan, appeared. This anthology, the *Hua-chien chi* (*Among the Flowers*), is characterized in the original preface as an attempt by some literati to improve the quality of the songs of the brothels. Independently, tz'u was also very popular around Nanking, at the court of the kingdom of the Southern T'ang (937–975).

There were enough informal channels for poets to come in contact with tz'u in the early days of the Sung dynasty that many did. Here was a new form, still largely oral—what could they do with it? They were, of course, writing poetry in the established forms al-

5

.

ready: to criticize the government, satirize enemies, communicate with friends, commemorate occasions, pass the time—and, above all, to pass the imperial examinations.

Though a century later tz'u would rival other forms for all these uses, save the examination, at the end of the tenth century it was used for themes appropriate to the singing house—banquets, gatherings of officials, festivals, outings—activities where "girls" and music were as essential as food and wine.

The poems translated here are arranged chronologically by author and begin with the late poems of Li Yü, last king of the Southern T'ang. His poems exerted an enormous influence over later tz'u imagery but they stand apart from early Sung tz'u, which were mostly about young women and love.

The appeal of tz'u—playful at first, more serious as time went on—must have been, in part, its very difference from its rival: the established and respected *shih* form. Shih traces its origins to the cornerstone of the Confucian classics, the *Shih ching* (*Book of songs*), an anthology supposedly compiled by Confucius.

One of the principal variants of shih that Sung poets inherited from the T'ang dynasty (618–907), new style (*chin-t'i*) shih, in its two most popular forms fixed the number of lines to four or eight, the number of words per line to consistently five or seven (Chinese is basically monosyllabic). Lines are end-stopped with a fixed caesura, and verbal parallelism is mandatory among lines in certain positions. Over time, much like Molière's Bourgeois Gentilhomme, who discovered that all his life he had been speaking prose, the Chinese had discovered that their language is tonal. About the fifth century the tones were isolated and classified. The effect on poetry in the T'ang, when new style developed, was dramatic. Rules about tonal parallelism—making the tonal sequence of one line opposite to that of the next—are integral to new style prosody, as are tonal restrictions to rhyme. "Dancing in shackles," one poet called it.

Sung poets handled this rigid and, to them, archaic shih form with great agility. Not only did they follow the rules, but they followed T'ang models so closely that they wrote, not in the language of their own time, but in the language as it had been in the early seventh century, and rhymed according to a dictionary compiled in 601. The language had changed sufficiently that it is not now clear how much of the new style shih they were writing could have been aurally appreciated even by the scholars themselves.

Tz'u by contrast was a wonderful new toy. It was in the then current language, comprehensible to anyone. In filling in tz'u, there were hundreds of tunes to choose from; old ones could be varied, new ones could be added. Length ranged from the shortest of sixteen words to the longest of two hundred and forty. Lines were of unequal lengths. Enjambment was allowed. There was no fixed caesura, little parallelism, considerable tonal variation within the line. Rhyme was less stringently linked to tone and in the current pronunciation.

The singing girls brought the music, the themes, the language, and probably the inspiration; the scholars, their refinement, intelligence, and skill. The combination produced highly personal lyrics that reflect the wit and imagination of the intelligentsia, expressed with a freshness and verve borrowed from the singers.

Imagine, then, how these songs might have been written and disseminated. Of the young singers who entertained the guests—all men and probably not too young—one, perhaps by her voice, her looks, her manner, or her song, would move an important minister. He, a literary man, corpulent if contemporary paintings are accurate, probably a little drunk, prided himself on his poetry: after all, he owed his position to this talent which had won him distinction

7

.

on the imperial examination. Stored in his memory was most of the great poetry of the past and many of the popular songs of the present. Her tune, too, most likely, was familiar.

To flatter the singer and divert the company, he would quickly write a new set of lyrics to her tune, following her rhymes, perhaps borrowing an expression here or there from her song or from one he had heard elsewhere, or from a well-known poem. She, on her part, aware that her fortunes were improved by the notice of this prominent man, would in future sing his tz'u. The lyrics he had filled in to her tune would, on other occasions, come to the attention of other officials, who would carry them from place to place as they migrated from one post to another. Three years was the official limit in one post.

Liaisons between a poet and particular singers were of varying degrees of transience. The poems are full of sorrowful partings, mostly described by men in the persona of a woman.

Even the highest ministers of state wrote in this tradition. In the charged, polarized, political atmosphere of the time, songs were occasionally used to discredit the opposition. Ou-yang Hsiu's enemies twice shattered his career using his tz'u as evidence of incest—most likely a trumped up charge, but indicative of the important role played by poetry. For the most part there were benign exchanges of poems, even between the fiercest of political enemies: Wang An-shih and Su Shih, for example, who admired one another's poems at the same time they ruthlessly opposed one another's policies.

Liu Yung and Su Shih, two widely different personalities, a generation apart—Liu, whose fame rests entirely on his tz'u, and Su who excelled at everything—were responsible for innovations that greatly enriched the form: Liu extended its length, Su its use. Liu Yung's move to longer forms, many of which he created himself,

8

appears to have been largely for metric and stylistic reasons: great-er variety of line lengths, more widely spaced rhythms. However, longer poems also allowed more description, changes of mood, emo-tional counterpoint, and more colloquial expression. Of the many thematic possibilities inherent in the expanded form, Liu himself tried few.

It was Su Shih, who, not much troubled by convention, used tz'u to express whatever he liked. He is variously credited and blamed for transforming tz'u from song into a literary form. Some said deri-sively that his tz'u were like shih; others said admiringly that he had broadened the scope of tz'u from a frivolity to an art.

Su—poet, painter, calligrapher, prose master, engineer, archi-tect, statesman, administrator, popular hero—put the details of his daily life, the entire spectrum of his interests, and the full weight of the tradition into tz'u. He wrote over three hundred, some exuber-ant, some melancholy, on a variety of subjects: personal, philosoph-ical, historical, and certainly not excluding the traditional tz'u theme of love. It is easy to see why as many people credit him with infusing new life into a form that would have faltered earlier as damn him for abusing it.

Within a very short time almost all the traditional shih themes appeared in tz'u: political protest, social comment, reportage. There were descriptions of paintings, scientific observation, trav-elogues, as well as reflections on history, old age, daily life. Auto-biography had been successfully tried both by Li Yü and Liu Yung. Most other themes were tried first by Su himself. From his time on, tz'u was divided into two schools: the heroic, or Su's, and the tradi-tional *Hua-chien chi,* which stuck to the themes of love and longing of that early anthology. Many later poets, as can be seen in these translations, wrote in both categories.

As the form's potential expanded, Sung poets wrote an increas-

9

·

ing proportion of tz'u. By Southern Sung (1127–1279), it was possible to be a heroic, patriotic poet and write tz'u exclusively, as Hsin Ch'i-chi did. Choice of form seems to have become simply a matter of personal preference. Liu Yung, had he lived then, could not have been dismissed as "simply a songwriter," as he had been a hundred years earlier, when shih was art and tz'u was pop.

Increased versatility did not affect tz'u's distinct character. It remained full of sights, colors, sounds, smells, and tastes, moving freely through time and space. Often an attribute is substituted for a noun—red for blossom, for example, is common. Consequently, one finds: broken red, fallen red, scattered red, remnants of red. Only slightly less frequent than metonymy is synecdoche—sail for boat, bridle for horse. Splashes of disembodied color and object fragments—abstract and surreal in themselves—are impressionistic in their use. Images are precise, tied to a specific moment, a season, a time of day, the experience of a particular person; the emotion, understated, or simply evoked. Visual images were so compelling they found their way not only into Chinese painting, but Japanese and Korean as well. Sung poets constructed from the details of their own lives a combination of landscape and self-portrait, half sketch, half diary.

Once tz'u had become as brilliant and many-faceted as the period itself, the perfect vehicle for the self-expression the Sung gentleman so passionately sought, each new use made it more usable.

Tz'u, which had originally meant "words to be sung," no longer needed to be sung at all. It became difficult to sing. Literary devices, such as subtitles, prose prefaces, allusion, quotation, became the norm rather than the exception. What had been partially a musical skill became almost completely a literary one. Famous old tunes that had been filled in for centuries disappeared completely and had to be replaced by patterns reconstructed from extant tz'u, described in terms of line length, tonal sequences, and rhyme. Tune titles, which had once evoked familiar melodies, became no more than names of meters. Occasionally someone revived the connection to music and even contributed new songs, notably Chou Pang-yen and Chiang K'uei. The trend, however, was away from music, from entertainment, from the popular to something more intellectual and classical.

The problems of translating Chinese poetry are legion, and begin with meaning. However precise the images, however clear the underlying emotion, what is actually being said may not be clear at all. The language has built-in ambiguities. There is no tense, no number, no case. Verbs are often omitted. Certain adjectives can function as verbs. Pronouns are rarely used; in poetry, virtually never. There is no Aristotelian commitment to a single point of view; there are no unities of time and place.

Punctuation is a modern phenomenon, unknown in the old texts, where poems are printed not line by line, but run-on, stanza by stanza. The end-stopped lines, verbal parallelism, and other structural elements of older forms help to decipher meaning. Tz'u has few semantic constraints and many formal options. These attributes—refreshing to the poets—help to make it even more obscure than other forms for the reader.

A three-character line, say, "this," "spring," "come," has dozens of possible meanings.

spring comes/is coming/has come
since spring came
when spring comes/came
if spring comes/were to come/had come

Spring, however, may not be the subject. There is no way of knowing whether the poet is talking about a change in the weather or somebody's visit. The line may have an implied pronoun, any pronoun.

He came in spring (or this spring)
If I had come in spring
When they came in spring
Since you came in spring
Were she to come in spring

Tense and pronoun can vary in each example. Enjambment from the preceding or to the following line would create other possibilities. Sometimes the context helps, often it merely compounds alternatives rather than solving ambiguities. Since borrowing lines, images, and conceits, far from being considered plagiarism, was thought elegant and erudite—quotation marks are not used—the whole line may have been quoted or paraphrased from another poem. This would add a new spectrum of meanings—provided, of course, that the source was extant, and that one recognized it.

Even the persona can change within a poem, and often seems to switch from one lover to the other in love poems. The line between gibberish and overinterpretation is thin. Intentional ambiguities are often hard to leave in, unintentional ones hard to take out.

These translations are printed line by line to preserve some sense of the rhythm, but I have omitted punctuation at the ends of lines. Internal punctuation is used sparingly. Lines are centered to render more visual one of the aspects of tz'u—whose other name in Chinese is "long and short line poetry." It also seemed somehow more suggestive of music—poems with the same tune titles should have a similar shape.

In early Sung, these titles identified the tune to which a particular poem was written. By late Sung, when much of the music had been lost, they identified the reconstructed metric patterns of those tunes. Structural differences between tz'u to one tune or another are significant. Someone might write twenty *P'u sa man,* almost as one might write twenty sonnets. As the names of little songs from the singing houses—"Bodhisattva Hairdo" or "Dotting the Lips"—are not so abstract as "sonnet" or "ode," to translate them might misleadingly suggest they refer to the content of the poem. They have therefore been left in transliterated form.

Tonal sequences are lost as English is not tonal. Though rhyme is important in the originals, I have not rhymed the translations because its effect in English is totally different. Chinese has many homophones, which make rhyming not only easier but less noticeable, since there is considerable natural accidental rhyme in the ordinary spoken language. In English rhyme easily sounds contrived and archaic, and would hardly make the translations sound colloquial.

In order to avoid footnotes, the famous stories most frequently alluded to are told in the following pages. As the stories are memorable, references to them in the poems should function for the English reader much as they were intended to for the Chinese.

It is as historical figures most of the poets represented here would be known to a Chinese reader: one was a king who lost his country, one an emperor who lost the empire, and one a woman who lost everything. The tendency of Chinese criticism has always been to intertwine the life and the work. Questions of meaning are resolved by reference to the life; questions of biography, by reference to the work. The two are then used circularly until all the details of each are complete. The whole package is passed from generation to generation, with the life—much of which has been factored out of the poems in the first place—as a sort of frame for the poems.

Li Yü's poems assume his story is known, allude to his life. To the

13

.

degree his story has been extrapolated from the poems in the first place, it is using the poems to intensify themselves.

In the case of Li Ch'ing-chao, the fact that she was a woman distorts much of the biographical material about her. As most Chinese love poetry is written by men in the persona of a woman, there was an unconscious inclination to fit Li—the person—to the stereotype of the persona.

Until the Ch'ing dynasty (1644–1911) there were practically no women writers, or perhaps their work was held of so little account it did not survive. Li is the venerated exception. Even for a woman of the scholar class, both by birth and by marriage, as Li was, education alone would have been unusual in Sung times. For all the many advances on every other front, the position of women took a great step backward. Footbinding became prevalent and made women virtual prisoners of the inner chambers; the resurgence of Confucian ideas created strong social pressure to keep them at their embroidery— illiterate. As neo-Confucianism became more and more important over the centuries, the scant known facts of Li Ch'ing-chao's life and the small amount of her surviving work were often interpreted—by her supporters—more to make her achievement morally and socially acceptable than to shed light on the work itself.

The case of Li Yü, therefore, indicates there is reason to look at biographical material to better appreciate the poems; that of Li Ch'ing-chao shows that such material should be approached with caution. Subtitles, indicating when, where, and why the poem was written, and, of course, the long autobiographical prose prefaces, suggest that for some poets context was important. By late Sung they provided it themselves.

If by limiting this selection to tz'u alone, something about tz'u as a genre is suggested in these translations, it is not by devising any methodology to find English equivalents for Chinese prosody, but by bringing together so many poems of one kind, by a handful of the most respected poets of a particular period. Sung aesthetics scorned superficial likeness. What was valued was something ineffable—the essence—and they sought to transmit its resonance. There was a great deal written in the Sung by the scholar-painter-poet-calligrapher on the subject of *ch'i* (essence, spirit) in the arts. The great Sung landscapes were not from nature, but distillations of nature. What was stressed over outward appearance—mere artisans, academy painters were called—was inner reality. "If there is no ch'i, then word is piled on word and nothing more."* The main reason to express this inner reality in painting, poetry and calligraphy—all viewed as aspects of the same thing—was to leave in the work the imprint of the individual mind.

---

* Yao Nai, quoted by David Pollard, "Ch'i in Chinese Literature," in Rickett, *Chinese Approaches to Literature*, p. 63.

Introduction to Symbols and Allusions

> *The poets from days of old have always followed in one another's steps from generation to generation. They refer to one another's experience and effect their own changes, and their success often comes from their being able to both accept and modify what has gone before.* LIU HSIEH (465–523)

Allusions, rare in early tz'u, were used increasingly after the twelfth century, eventually to excess. Nevertheless, all the poems included here are accessible. Time could not fade them, nor do their roots in an alien culture make them obscure.

The literate in China were, however, for millennia, a homogeneous group. They studied the same classics, memorized the same poems, led similar lives. In this context a few words could do anything from play cleverly with a well-known image to evoke another situation that, by contrast or comparison, might add a new dimension to the poem.

To flag and explain what an outsider might miss makes too much of the substance of allusion, when the power of allusion is not in its substance but in its ability to suggest, to evoke images that will resonate in some nonspecific way with those explicit in the poem. Not all, but most references depend on only a handful of symbols, a few

Shih, Vincent Yu-chung, trans. *The Literary Mind and the Carving of the Dragons*, p. 249.

stories. It seems possible, therefore, to bring the reader far enough into the culture to decide what is being evoked and why. To that end a few stories are told here, a few symbols identified.

The Chinese of the Sung dynasty lived close to nature. Times of the day, times of the year, plants, animals, the sun, the moon, the stars—all are important. The simplest symbols, therefore, come from nature.

Flowers and blossoms in their ephemeral and transient beauty suggest women and, by extension, the passage of time. Plum blossoms, which generally bloom first, alone and in a snowy landscape, imply loneliness and seclusion as well. These suggestions appear in many guises. Su Shih in the "Willow Flower" tz'u describes the flower as if it were a woman. In his tz'u to the tune *Ho hsin lang,* the persona, a woman, identifies with the trembling pomegranate blossoms. Ou-Yang Hsiu's lines, "Drunk among the flowers" or "Buying a flower, like wine, in the Ch'ang-an market," though euphemistic to a degree, genuinely talk of flowers at the same time that they suggest courtesans. By and large the connections are subtle and fluid.

Although the secluded willow tree is a frequent symbol for a woman, the willow spray suggests parting. It was the custom from early times to break a small branch in farewell. Willows seem routinely to have been planted at the landings along rivers and dykes from which members of the vast bureaucratic army set off for different posts.

Other trees with symbolic significance were the *wu-t'ung* and the banana palm. The wu-t'ung, the last to lose its leaves in autumn, epitomizes fall, the passage of time, the end of profusion, fragrance, and sometimes youth. The banana, known for the sorrowful sound

18

of rain on its large leaves, is sometimes itself a symbol of sorrow. It "resonates anguish, separation," wrote Li Ch'ing-chao.

Among the birds, there are the ubiquitous mandarin ducks (*yüan-yang*) girls and young women are forever embroidering, particularly on bridal quilts. They stand for conjugal felicity. Swallows, which tend to keep the same mate, symbolize fidelity. Because they are also migrant, their comings and goings, like those of geese, note a change of season, the passage of time. Their freedom to go back is often contrasted to the plight of the person watching them, who longs to return but cannot.

Wild geese are the traditional messengers, both because their formation in flight denotes a Chinese character and from the story of Su Wu (c. first century B.C.), imprisoned by the Hsiung-nu for nineteen years, who sent a message home, tied to the foot of a migrating wild goose. Geese are a favorite symbol for Li Ch'ing-chao: "The geese have passed / I'm left ten thousand thoughts unsent."

The cuckoo and partridge, the nightjar, the goatsucker (in all varieties: *che-ku, t'i-chüeh, t'i-kuei, tu-chüan*) cry at equinox, the end of spring. Their cry is onomatopoetic for "you can't go home." The chirp of the cricket is also onomatopoetic: *chi-chi,* "cold, cold"— *ch'u-ch'u,* "wrong, wrong."

The roc (*p'eng*), a fabulous bird of enormous size, mounts upon a great wind, to a height of ninety thousand li, and flies for six months to the Southern Ocean. It is associated with immortality. The story is originally from Chuang-tzu.

As for the moon, it is well to remember the Chinese calendar is lunar. Festivals, consequently, are associated with phases of the moon. When full the moon unites the gaze of people who are separated. Separations are particularly poignant at Moon Festival in the middle of the eighth lunar month (approximately mid-autumn),   19
                                                                        .

when the custom is to view the full moon with those close to you, not necessarily a lover. Some of the nicest poems on this theme, written on Moon Festival, are by Su Shih, thinking of his younger brother, Tzu-yu: "Life on this night is not often good." The brothers maintained a strong attachment throughout their lives but were almost permanently separated. Poems, a popular form of correspondence among intellectuals of the Sung, were frequently exchanged.

Another full moon festival is the first full moon of the new year, Lantern Festival (First Full Moon, Upper January, or more precisely, the mid-point of the first lunar month). The atmosphere is of a carnival, replete with romance, trysts, and flirtation. It was one of the rare occasions when women could leave the inner chambers. Music, entertainment, vendors of all sorts, a flower market—the whole population in the streets—the festival lasted three days and three nights. Streets were ablaze with paper lanterns in flower, fish, and dragon shapes.

In the moon the Chinese see a rabbit, a toad, and a laurel tree. Ch'ang O fled there with the elixir of immortality, stolen from her husband. She is the moon goddess, and lives there with an attendant population of ethereal beings.

Among the stars, those most frequently referred to are the Herd Boy and the Weaving Maid, once lovers, now constellations separated by the River of Stars (River of Heaven, Silver River), our Milky Way. The lovers meet once a year, the seventh day of the seventh month, over a bridge of magpies. On this day, a festival, girls displayed their embroidery.

Cold Hearth Festival, sometimes called Cold Food Festival or The Day of No Fire, commemorates the burning of a wise man by a foolish monarch, but is almost always simply a reference to the sea-

20

.

son in which it occurs, the end of spring. "A thousand flowers strew the path to Cold Hearth Festival," writes Ou-yang Hsiu. Old fires were extinguished and remained so for several days, before the ceremonial "new fire" was kindled and passed from torch to torch. Cold Hearth Festival immediately precedes Ch'ing-ming—devoted to sweeping the graves of the ancestors and going into the country to enjoy nature.

Often references to famous stories or poems are so subtle and so closely woven into the poem they could easily go unnoticed. Chang Hsien's phrase, "Ageless heaven," is a distillation of a line by the T'ang poet Li Ho (791–817), "If heaven had feelings, it too would age." Lu Yu refers to the same line by inverting the conceit: "If heaven weren't indifferent I would ask / How it can bear to turn a lover gray?"

The Chinese have an elaborate taste for metonymy and synecdoche. If we in the west wanted to suggest jealousy by a reference to Othello, would dropping a handkerchief be enough? Tz'u, particularly after Su Shih, is full of this type of shorthand. The stories were so well known and well used that mention of even a trivial element evoked the whole.

"Leaning against the rail," is one such example, from a poem of Li Yü, first poet represented in this collection. He was the last king of Southern T'ang, imprisoned by the first Sung emperor, kept under house arrest, alone, in an alien landscape, remembering, regretting. After two years, legend has it, he was poisoned on his forty-second birthday by a bottle of wine sent by the second Sung emperor. He left a handful of the most beautiful, autobiographical poems in the language. Climbing the high tower, leaning against the rail, became frequent images in Sung tz'u; they evoke his story.

In an early Han rhyme-prose composition, the *Kao t'ang fu*, Sung

21

Yü, a courtier to King Hsiang of Ch'u (r. 298–265 B.C.) is traveling with the king and tells him the following story:

> Once a former king journeyed to Kao-t'ang. He became weary and took a nap. He dreamt he saw a woman who said, "I am the lady of Wu Mountain, and I am a guest at Kao-t'ang. I heard you were traveling here and I wished to offer you the pillow and the mat." The king favored her, and leaving she said to him: "I live on the southern side of the Wu Mountain in rocky crags of Kao-ch'iu. At dawn I am the morning cloud, at dusk, the driving rain."
>
> Lois Fusek, trans., *Monumenta Serica*, (1972–73), 30:413

Over time, any aspect of this story or place in the region became a euphemism for a love affair or sexual encounter: Wu Mountain, Yang-t'ai (the terrace where the meeting took place), Ch'u Gorge (also in the vicinity), K'ao-t'ang, King Hsiang, and, at times, clouds and rain. Mention of Sung Yü himself, however, is apt to be in a different context. He was thought to be a follower of Ch'ü Yüan (322–295 B.C.), a poet-official who drowned himself when his sovereign failed to make use of his services, and to whom is attributed the major portion of one of the earliest anthologies, the *Ch'u tz'u* (*Songs of the South*). Sung Yü, therefore, is a symbol of sorrow and disappointment. All of these allusions are frequent in Liu Yung.

The rejected woman is often suggested by reference to Long Gate. When Empress Ch'en lost favor with Han Wu-ti (r. 140–86 B.C.), she was sent in a green cart to Long Gate. From there, she bribed the poet Ssu-ma Hsiang-ju with a hundred catties of gold to write a *fu* (a rhyme-prose composition) describing her grief, which would regain for her the favor of the emperor. He did, and it did. It is known as the fu of Long Gate. Whether Long Gate was actually a palace for retired concubines or not, that is the image it evokes in poetry.

Long Gate, the fu by Ssu-ma Hsiang-ju, one hundred catties of gold, the green cart—mention of any one of these alludes to this story and can refer either to a rejected woman or a rejected minister. Buying a fu, or "even with a hundred catties of gold" stand for attempts at reconciliation.

Anyone familiar with Chinese painting will know the story of Wang Chao-chün (also known as Wang Ch'iang or Ming-fei), courtesan under Han Yüan-ti (r. 48–32 B.C.), "she whose horse carried sorrow 30,000 li." According to legend, it was the custom of the emperor to select among his concubines from portraits. To attract attention, therefore, the ladies bribed the artist to create a portrait more dazzling than its subject. Wang Chao-chün refused to do this. She was either too proud or too poor. As a result, she was never noticed by the emperor, who eventually gave her to a Hsiung-nu chieftain to cement a peace treaty. When she came into the imperial presence to take her leave, he realized what he had missed. It was too late.

She is in many poems and paintings making her sad journey out of China, past the great wall to the steppe to live among the barbarians. About the third century she began to be pictured on horseback singing to the p'i-p'a, a stringed instrument similar to a lute. There is a legend, too, that her grave in the desert is always green. Sung poets would probably have thought of her as she is pictured by the T'ang poet, Tu Fu:

Lament Among the Ruins

Countless peaks, ten thousand valleys, converge on Ching Gate
The village where Ming-fei was born

Once she was sent from the Purple Palace to the desert
There a green grave remains in the dusk
Her portrait—the face of a spring breeze
Yet the jangle of jade follows a ghost
A thousand years the Tartar lute
Will sing her sad reproach

Hers is the quintessential sorrow of exile.

The five-stringed lute refers to Ching K'o, one of the "Assassin-Retainers" whose story appears in the *Shih chi* (*Records of the Grand Historian*) of Ssu-ma Ch'ien (145–86 B.C.). When the state of Yen was in danger of being swallowed by Ch'in, which had already taken several neighboring states, Ching K'o was hired by the prince of Yen to assassinate the king of Ch'in. The Yen court accompanied Ching K'o on his suicidal mission as far as the banks of the Yi River. There, dressed in mourning—white—they gave him a farewell banquet, and to the five-stringed lute he sang:

The wind sighs, sighs
            Yi waters run cold
The hero once gone
            Will not return

This, in Hsin Ch'i-chi becomes:

At the Yi, to the sighs of a cold west wind
They gathered in white mourning like the snow
To hear the destined hero's tragic song, still incomplete

A popular story of the same era, recorded in the same source, concerns a famous general, Lien P'o. The king of Chao, another enemy of Ch'in, sent Feng T'ang to see whether the general was too old to serve. To prove he was still hale the general consumed a great deal of rice. Asking whether someone can still eat rice is another way of asking if he is too old to serve. Su Shih, in "Hunting in Mi-chou," asks:

> When will the emperor send Feng T'ang
> So I can stretch my bow into the full moon
> Gaze north
> And shoot the Sky Wolf?

In other words, when will the emperor find out I'm still worth my salt? The Sky Wolf, incidently, is a constellation associated with rebellion.

A slightly later story, also political, concerns Chang Han (c. 258–319) and is told by Liu I-ch'ing (403–444) in the *Shih-shuo hsin-yü* (*A New Account of the Tales of the World*). Chang Han, an official serving in Loyang, was reminded by a gust of autumn wind of the seasonal delicacies of his home in Kiangsu: lu fish and seaweed. On this pretext he resigned and went home. The moral is to leave office before the tide of imperial favor shifts. The allusion is popular with Hsin Ch'i-chi:

> Seek repose in time—
> No, not simply for the taste of seaweed and lu fish
> When autumn settles on the river
> See how the geese evade the bow strings
> Returning boats avoid the backwash?

From the colorful period of the Three Kingdoms (221–280) come many heroes and allusions. After the fall of the Han dynasty (206 B.C.–A.D. 220), three kingdoms, Shu in the southwest, Wu in the south, and Wei in the north, vied for supremacy to reunify the em-

25

pire. The intrigues and counterintrigues of this period read like a cross between *The Three Musketeers* and *A Tale of Two Cities*. The geographical division of China into these three areas has persisted in literature long after they lost any political relevance.

Ts'ao Ts'ao, commander of Wei, who did eventually establish a short-lived dynasty, suffered a terrible defeat in the war's most famous battle at Red Cliff. There, Chou Yü, the commanding general for King Sun Ch'üan of Wu, by a clever stratagem, burned Ts'ao's fleet and decimated his army. Because they were married to the king and his general, two famous beauties, sisters named Ch'iao, are often mentioned, occasionally just to refer to a woman. The Wu capital, Nanking, admired for its scenery and as a natural fortress—ringed by mountains, the river forming a natural moat—served as capital for a number of dynasties. Allusions to the Three Kingdoms are popular with Su Shih, Chou Pang-yen, and Hsin Ch'i-chi.

Though these stories resonate in some of the poems that follow, it is not always clear in what sense they are evoked. The name of a historical figure is sometimes little more than a way for the poet to refer to himself. Even those images originally based on historical facts, as literary images, underwent changes with each new use.

For the Chinese poet, all earlier poetry was contemporary. He is apt to answer a poem written centuries earlier as though it had come in today's mail. So Chiang K'uei, seeing Chu-hsi three centuries after Tu Mu wrote about it, answers Tu's poems. In a few of these instances I have added the early poems just after the tz'u that evokes them. The literate in the Sung dynasty would probably have known them by heart.

26

.

Poems

Yü mei jen

Spring flowers, autumn moon, when will they end?
Of what once was, what's left?
Upstairs last night there was an east wind
Unbearable, in bright moonlight, to look back

Carved railings, jade walkways, should be there still
Only youth has gone
How much more sorrow is to come?
It is a river, fed by spring rain, flowing east

NTECT 9

LI YÜ

Wu yeh t'i

Last night, wind and rain
In bamboo curtains, sounds of autumn
The candle sputters, the water clock drips, I toss and turn
Get up, sit down—no peace

World affairs flow, spread, like spilled water
And life? A drifting dream
The land of the drunk, that's secure, go there
Elsewhere, it's not worth the walk

Tzu yeh

Sorrow, regret—who can avoid them?
I alone am consumed
Always going back to my country in dreams
Waking in tears

Who now will climb the high tower with me?
Or still remember bright autumn, there—
The past is already empty
A dream

NTECT 13

Wang chiang nan

What pain!
Last night I dreamed
Nothing had changed, I rambled palace gardens
Coaches flowing like water, my horse a dragon
Flowers, moonlight, and a spring breeze!

NTECT 18

Ch'ing p'ing yüeh

We part, spring is half finished
Everything my eye caresses breaks my heart
On the steps, it's snowing plum blossoms
Brush them off, you are covered again

Geese come, but bring no news
The way back is long, impossible, even in dreams
The sorrow of parting spreads like spring grass
On and on, still it grows

NTECT 19 *

Hsiang chien huan

Spring red has faded from the forest flower
Too soon, too soon
Chill morning rain and evening wind can not be stayed

Tears tinged with rouge
Held me, drunk
When again?
Since then, life has been long, a river of regrets, flowing east

NTECT 24 •

Lang t'ao sha

The past weighs, brings only sorrow
Here, how can I escape it?
Autumn wind, and in the court, moss on the steps
A single strand of bead curtain, not free to blow
All day alone

The gold sword, already lost, buried
My soul a jungle of weeds
Cool evening, tranquil sky, the moon rising
I think of the jade towers that cast long shadows
Into the Ch'in-huai—in vain

NTECT 39

Yü mei jen

Soft winds return to the small yard, dry weeds turn green again
The blossoming willow heralds another spring
I languish half the day, silent, alone
Whispering bamboo, new moon, are as they were

Before the music ended—and the wine—
When ice on the pool began to melt
Perfume permeated the palace, aglow with candles
Now, frost covers the snow on my temples—how could I not remember?

NTECT 40˙

P'o chen tzu

Four decades of home and country
Three thousand li of mountains, rivers
Phoenix pavilions, dragon towers, tracing a high horizon
Lush wisteria embracing sculptured jade—
What use had we for the arts of war?

Suddenly I am nothing, a captive
I waste my days growing thin, gray
Rue my frenzied abdication at the shrine
Court musicians playing the farewell
Tears falling before the gathered palace girls

NTECT 47 (DISPUTED)

Lang t'ao sha

Outside the bamboo curtain, rain, rain
Spring fades
Silk covers can not withstand the early morning cold
Within a dream, my body forgets it is a prisoner:
A flash of greedy pleasure

Not alone, leaning by the rail
Mountains and rivers beyond count
Parting was easy, compared to trying to go back
Petals fall, in flowing water spring passes—
To heaven? Or on to others?

NTECT 49

Yü fu

Froth on the waves—a thousand snow drifts
Peach and plum, mute troop of spring—
A bottle of wine
A rod—a strike!
What luck—can any match it?

NTECT 56 * (DISPUTED)

41

·

LI YÜ

Yü fu

Only an oar, a spring breeze, a skiff
A strand of silk and a light hook
Islets full of flowers
Goblet full of wine
Amid ten thousand waves, what freedom!

NTECT 57 (DISPUTED)

LI YÜ

Hsiang chien huan

Silent, alone, I climb the west tower
The moon a hook
Quiet, secluded, the wu-t'ung, clear autumn locked into the court

Cut it, it does not sever
Sort it, it ravels more
The sorrow of parting—
A taste—a weight . . .

NTECT 63 *

Hsiang szu ling

Wu mountains are green
Yüeh mountains are green
Two banks of green mountains: one sees you off, the other beckons
Who knows what you feel as you go?

You full of tears
I full of tears
But we've not yet knotted the silken cord
And the tide is ready . . .

CST 7[*]

Tien chiang ch'un

In Golden Valley, year after year
Spring grows helter-skelter—who decides
Where petals fall
And mixed with misty rain, blanket the earth?

Farewell songs again
As the gates of the post station close at dusk
You go—
Things madly growing
Every which way along the road

CST 7

47

·

LIN PU

Shuang t'ien hsiao chiao

Clear ice, fresh frost
Last night the plum blossomed—
Where was the jade flute that three times
Haltingly hung melody among the moonlit branches?

Dreams end
When incense burns out
Daybreak is cold, orchid wood, just ash—
Roll up the blinds—let me enjoy the stillness
Don't sweep the snow from the steps just yet

CST 7

48
·

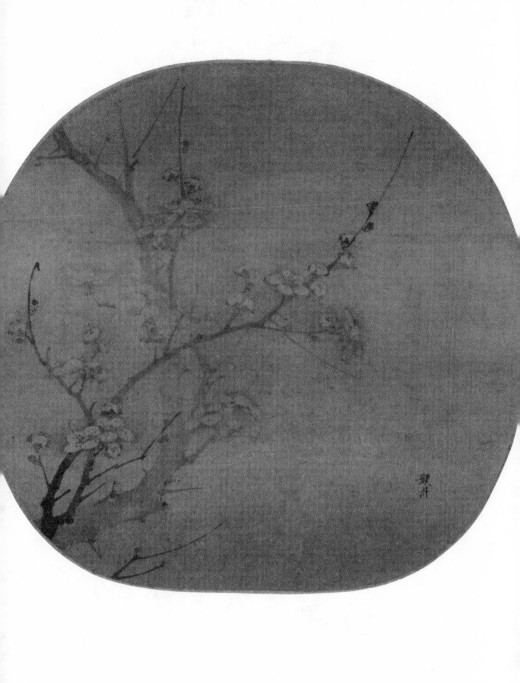

Su mu che

Nostalgia

Dark clouds in the sky
Yellow leaves on the ground
A wash of autumn color right to the sea
And on the waves a cold green mist
Shafts of sunlight play with sky and mountains in the water
The fragrant grass has no sympathy—
It's still untouched by the setting sun

Gloom far from home
Stalks the traveler
Night after night, unless
A pleasant dream hold him in sleep—
Oh don't, in bright moonlight, lean idly in the tower, alone
Wine to a sad heart
Turns to tears of longing

CST 11

FAN CHUNG-YEN

Yü chia ao

Autumn Thoughts

In autumn the scene by the great wall changes
The geese go to Heng-yang—they wouldn't think of staying
On all sides, the horn sparks sounds of the frontier that echo
And fill a thousand mountains
Mists roll in, the sun sets, the isolated city closes its gates

I drink a cup of muddy wine ten thousand miles from home
The record of our victory still blank: no hope of going back
Long drawn notes on a tartar flute, frost—
The men are restless
A white haired general sheds a soldier's tears

CST 11

Yü chieh hsing

One by one falling leaves scatter on the fragrant step
Disturbing the still night
With brittle rustlings
I raise the pearl curtain in the empty jade tower
The Silver River cascades to earth from a clear sky
Year after year such nights
When the moon flowers like washed silk
He is still a thousand miles away

Too miserable even to drink—
Before I touch the wine it turns to tears . . .
The dying lamplight flickers, I lie down
To sleep alone—a taste all too familiar
That's all love comes to—
This weight on my brow and heart—
I can't get away from it!

CST II

FAN CHUNG-YEN

Tsui ch'ui pien

Two silk butterflies played on her skirt
When first I saw her at the east pond feast
In light make-up
A casual flower of early spring

The more I look, the more I find perfection—
Her willow waist, the talk of all—
Yesterday at dusk, she put the mountains in disorder
When she came, trailing the clouds

CST 57

54

·

CHANG HSIEN

Yi ts'ung hua ling

Grief and longing up in the tower—do they ever end?
No burden like love
From the skein of parting come a thousand disordered threads
Intensified along the eastern path
By a drizzle of catkins
The neigh of his horse fades in the distance
Pleasure without end—
What trace of it is left?

Ducks in pairs drift on the smooth pond
A small oar cuts through from the south
Setting sun, ladder pulled up by the storied pavilion
Again the curtains hide the slanting moon
She broods about love lost
And envies peach and apricot
Scattering as if to marry the east wind

CST 61

55

CHANG HSIEN

T'ien hsien tzu

Water Melody

*Written when I was a minor official in Chia-ho, home
sleeping instead of at the office, because I was sick.*

I listened to a few bars of the water melody as I drank
And woke from that noon wine, still in the grip of sorrow
Spring—I watched it go, it's gone—when will it come again?
Evening already faces me from the mirror
Too bad it all passes
Beyond recapture

On the sandbar, two birds, on the pond, gathering darkness
The moon breaks through the clouds, flowers dance with their shadows
Layer after layer of curtains hide the lamplight
The restless wind
While I sleep
Will, by tomorrow, strew the path with petals

CST 70

CHANG HSIEN

Ch'ien ch'iu sui

A nightjar's calls
Again herald an end to fragrance, profusion
Poor spring—what's left of red to pluck?
Rain and light wind have cruelly changed her aspect
To the season of green plums
At Yung-feng, willows—
Not a soul about all day—let fly a blizzard of catkins

Oh don't take up the subtle strings and play!
Their brooding could move
Ageless heaven
Desire never ends
The heart, like a tangled web
Has a thousand knots
Nights pass
And the east window, not yet light, frames the chill remnant of a moon

CST 72

57
.

CHANG HSIEN

Mu lan hua

Cold Hearth Festival, 1075

Dragon boat races draw young men in Wu
On bamboo swings, girls frolic in pairs
The shoal, fragrant with grasses to pick—no thought to home till dusk—
We come and go pell-mell, dishevelling the wild lush green

Clouds disperse, remote hills are dark
Music and singing have ended, it's quiet by the garden pool
Moonlight floods the courtyard
Countless catkins drift, casting no shadow

CST 75

58
·

CHANG HSIEN

Ch'ing men yin

Suddenly nice again after the chill
Wind and rain clearing at last by evening
The garden desolate as Ch'ing-ming nears
And I, drunk, among the battered flowers—
Same agony as years ago

Roused by the sound of wind through the cornice
At night, when all is still behind the many layered doors
How can I stand it? Bright moonlight
Sends the shadow of her swing over the garden wall

CST 83

CHANG HSIEN

P'u sa man

A keening lute plays the Hsiang River song
Note by note it sketches the Hsiang's green waves
Delicate fingers compel the thirteen strings
To cruel regret

First slowly, like flowing water
Then, over the jade bridges like flying wild geese
She plays to the point of heartbreak
And her black eyebrows follow the form of mountains in spring

CST 85 •

60
•

Huan ch'i sha

Same song, new words, one cup of wine
Last year's air still lingers on the terrace
The evening sun sets in the west—when will you return?

Petals fall—how could one stay them?
The swallows that we knew are back again
Alone I watch the ebb and flow along the garden path

CST 89

·

YEN SHU

Huan ch'i sha

Youth doesn't last
Even trivial separations take their toll
Don't miss a chance to dance and sing!

Why fill your gaze with mountains and rivers, pining for one far away?
Falling flowers, wind and rain, will ruin spring the more—
Better just love the one who's near

CST 90

63
•

YEN SHU

Ch'üeh t'a chih

By the fence, chrysanthemums grieve—mist, dew—orchids weep
Through the silk curtains comes a slight chill
And the swallows leave, two by two
What does the moon know of bitter parting—
When it still drives bright shafts through the red door until dawn?

Last night a west wind withered green trees
Alone I climb the high tower
Gaze to the road's end at the edge of heaven
If only I could send colorful letters, white silk
Beyond the mountains and rivers—but where?

CST 91

64
·

Ch'ing p'ing yüeh

On red paper in a fine hand
She tells all the feelings of her life
But with the geese in the clouds, the fish in the water
What hope is there of sending them?

At sunset, alone, in the west chamber
Distant mountains are just beside the curtain hook
But to see his face, where should she turn?
Green waves flow as before, still east

CST 92

65

.

YEN SHU

Ch'ing p'ing yüeh

Gently the autumn wind
Shakes leaf after leaf from the wu-t'ung
At the first taste of green wine, drunk
I rest my head against the window in thick sleep

Indigo and red of myrtle and hibiscus fade
Late sun lingers along the rail
It's time the swallows thought of leaving
The silver screen last night felt chill

CST 92

66

·

YEN SHU

Mu lan hua

After the swallows and the geese pass, the orioles go
Carefully I number the tangled threads of this short life
Hardly longer than a spring dream
It disappears like autumn clouds beyond recall

Music of the ch'in can charm, but once the goddess unties her ornaments
You cannot hold her, even if you rend her silks
Don't be the only one who's sober
When you could count with those dead drunk among the flowers

CST 95

YEN SHU

Mu lan hua

The water in the pond was green, the wind a little warm
When first I saw her—
To the ring of the melody's opening bars
She came dancing, waist spinning red confusion

Beneath the rail's jade arabesques, there by the fragrant steps
We drank so much we didn't know the sun had set
Then you were there—
Now, less than half of us are left!

CST 96

T'a so hsing

Along the path, red is scarce
The whole fragrant countryside is green—
See the high tower densely shaded by trees?
The spring wind doesn't know to stop the catkins blowing
They shower in your face, pell-mell, as you walk

Green leaves hide the oriole
Red screens obscure the swallows
Slowly incense smoke rises in tangled threads . . .
Once awake from wine's sad dream
The day's last slanting rays already shine deep in the court

CST 99

69
·

T'a so hsing

After the songs of parting
And the farewell banquet
Fragrant dust already between us, I still look back—
You stay—the cry of your lone horse echoes through the forest
I go—my oar follows the waves

Secluded, ornate rooms, soul consumed with longing—
From the high tower, eyes try the limits of space
The setting sun can send its shimmer only so far
But the sorrow of parting is without end
It fills the earth to the edge of heaven

<small>CST 99</small>

•

YEN SHU

Shan t'ing liu

For the Singer

She came from Western Chin
With nothing—trusting to a modest flair
For willow flower songs
Competing for the sharp and new
By chance she mastered Nien-nu's tone and pitch
At times so high it held the moving clouds
Shu silk beyond measure rewarded
Her struggle

Years passed, on the roads of Hsien-yang
She wore herself out for dregs of wine, food gone cold
And how she felt
Whom could she tell?
If there were even one who understood
She would not grudge a single note, even of *Sunny Spring*—
Once, when she sang before the guests, their tears fell
Now it is she who hides behind silk sleeves

CST 106

Yü lou ch'un

Hating Spring

Among green willows and fragrant grass along the road of post stations
Youth discards you and slips away
In the tower the fifth watch bell shatters what's left of dreams
Beneath the blossoms, the sorrow of parting and March rain

More bitter to love than not—
One inch unravels to a thousand, ten thousand threads
Somewhere is an edge of heaven, an end of earth
But to longing, there is no end

CST 108

P'o chen tzu

The day the swallows come, spring begins
After the pear blossoms fall, it's Ch'ing-ming
On the pond a few specks of green
Under the leaves, the yellow oriole chirps a note or two
All day long the catkins fly

The girl from next door comes giggling
We meet picking mulberry leaves along the path
No wonder I had such a good spring dream last night—
Today my fighting grass beats hers
Smiles grow on both cheeks

CST 108

YEN SHU

Tieh lien hua

Green trees lean against the curved rail
A gentle breeze stirs the willows
Scattering golden threads
Who plays the cheng
And sends a pair of sea swallows flying through the screen?

Everywhere willow strands and falling catkins in confusion
When red apricots blossom
It's almost time for Ch'ing-ming rains
Awakened from thick sleep by the orioles aimless chatter
I can not find the remnant of my startled dream

CST 109 * (DISPUTED)

YEN SHU

Ch'ü yü kuan

Among the peaks, clouds fly
Along the riverbank, the sun lingers
Upstairs, by the rail, day in day out, mist and wave all she sees
One look toward the deserted passes where the river flows
A thousand miles of clear autumn
Afflict the eye

There, far far from the capital
And from the fresh, soft, lovely girl
Who, since they parted waits for letters that don't come
The geese, treacherous messengers
Fly slowly past along the shoal
Trailing long thoughts

Secretly, from the beginning, she dreamed only
Of trysts, illicit pleasures—how many would there be?
What did she know of meeting, parting? Waiting is a misery
Past happiness turns to rain, past love to sorrowful clouds
To follow is made impossible
When he leaves—climbs the mountains, goes down to the river—
It starts again, the day to day of love—
A void, consuming, black
Long hours without speaking
And nothing for it but to come down from the tower

CST 17

76
•

LIU YUNG

Yü lin ling

Chilled by the cicadas' dirge
We reach the post station at evening
Just after a sudden shower—
The banquet toasts at the gate seemed endless—
Here, where we long to linger, the boat impels you to be off
You take my hands—I see your tears through mine
Words, futile now, catch in my throat
I think of your going on and on—a thousand li of mist and wave—
How dense the evening clouds, how wide the Ch'u sky!

To love and part—what age old anguish
How can I bear clear autumn's desolation too
Not knowing where you'll wake from wine tonight?
The willows along the bank
The breeze at dawn, a fading moon—
Without you, the passing year—
Moments, scenery—all wasted
Were they to rouse a thousand subtle feelings
Who'd understand?

CST 21

Ts'ai lien ling

Soft moonlight dissolves
Into a frosty dawn—
Cruel moment for the west bound traveler—
Lovely the girl who takes his hand
To see him to the crossing; the red doors sigh and open
A thousand such fine faces, fair and gentle, wait for him—
Without a word, she sheds her tears
Sick at heart, he tries not to look back

A skiff of orchid wood
Is poised with convenient urgency to take the tides
He's eager to be off
How would he know the threads of parting
By the thousands, in her disordered heart?
Or the taste of bitterness in a silence she can not share?
Still, he turns—once city walls are out of sight—
Beyond the cold river and sky
Half hidden, stand two three misty trees

CST 23

Feng hsi wu

Waiting expectantly high in the tower in a slim breeze
I see to the reaches of space—only spring sorrow
Growing, dark, dark, to the edge of heaven
The sunset on the mist colors the grass
Words are useless—who would understand why I linger by the rail?

I should have one mad fling, get drunk—
"When there's wine, sing"—
But forced joy has no flavor
My belt grows loose—never mind
I'm pale and worn—she's worth it!

CST 25

Lang t'ao sha man

Startled from dreams by a thread of wind
That has blown out the lamp and left it cold
She dreads awakening from wine
To hear again the drip of rain against the empty step
Alas, he lingers at the ends of earth so long
She is betrayed—his vows lie shattered!
How could he let the joys of yesterday
Turn in no time into this misery?

In deep despair
She relives, again and again
Their first night
The banquet over, the songs ended
The warm fragrance of the yüan-yang quilt—
Briefly together, quickly parted—
And now she squanders youth
In dreams of passion
There are a thousand—ten thousand kinds
Of love and longing

From then till now
So much time passed
Cast off for no reason
When to make love again?
She dreams of lowering the shade, a shared pillow—
Soft whispers—
Night after night in the village by the river
Cold again, going over it all, again . . .

Ting feng po

Spring came
Cruel green and vexing red
Who cares? Not I!
When the sun rises above the blossoms
And orioles weave through the willows
I'm still asleep
Warm glow fading
Bright hair limp
All day I drag about, uncombed
So what?
Hateful the casual lover who just leaves
And sends no word, no letter

I knew it would be like this
Now I'm sorry that from the start
I didn't lock up your fancy saddle
And by the study window
Give you fine paper and an ivory brush
Make you recite and do your work
And follow you all day
Not let you go!
I'd fool with thread and needle, sit by you
And you by me—
Not throw my youth away!

CST 29

81

·

Shao nien yu

The horse dallies on the Ch'ang-an road
High in the willows, a reckless cicada cries
Sunset beyond the islands
Autumn winds rising on the plain
Darkness closes in, cuts me off

Clouds, once they go, are gone
Where now will I find you again?
I've no desire for someone new
Even drinking seems futile, empty—
Not like last year

CST 32

82
·

LIU YUNG

Ch'i shih

Late autumn sky
A sudden shower sprinkles the yard
A few scraggly chrysanthemums linger by the door
The wu-t'ung by the well, disheveled
Entices the remaining mist
What misery!
Looking at the water and the mountain passes
Clouds flying across a lazily setting sun
I feel Sung Yü's despair
When, reaching the river, he saw the ranges to be crossed
Along the endless road that is
The wanderer's bane
I'm sick of the Lung River's clang and bang
The cicadas cry among the rotten leaves
The crickets crick in decaying grasses
Noise answering noise

In lonely inns a day goes like a year
Wind and dew gradually change
Quietly, late at night
The long sky clears
Limpid and shallow the River of Stars
Washed in bright moonlight . . .
Thoughts churning
Through the long night, looking at all this
How can I bear furtively to recall times past?
With neither fame nor office

83
·

Lingering along the lovely path to the red tower
I squandered the years

The capital was beautiful
And I was young
Banquets at night, love in the morning
Wild friends, bizarre companions—
Singing and drinking—
Each tried to be the last to leave
In the flash of a shuttle, it was over
And now past revels seem a dream
What limit to the mist and water along the road?
Brooding over old promise, wealth, and name, unmans me—
To think back is misery, for nothing
It's late
I feel the chill
Slowly the painted horn sighs a few last notes
I turn to the window
Put out the lamp and face another dawn
Embracing my own shadow—again no sleep

CST 35

Wang hai ch'ao

The whole southeast is splendid
And of the cities of Chiang Wu
Ch'ien-t'ang has always been outstanding
Misty willows adorn the bridges
Screen the wind, drape them green—
A hundred thousand houses, big and small—
Trees reach the clouds along the sand embankment
Angry waves froth like snow
In a boundless natural moat—
Pearls and jewels in the market
Behind each door, silks and satins
Excess vies with extravagance

Layers of clear lakes, lovely hills
Toward the end of autumn, osmanthus
Ten li of flowering lotus
On a fine day, pipes play
Songs drift from the boats at night
Old men, fishing, laugh with young girls gathering lotus
Here, a thousand horsemen massed behind a noble standard
And, drunk, stopped to listen to flute and drum
Chant poems praising mist and cloud—
Some day I'll brag about the scenery—
Go back to Feng-ch'ih, and brag!

CST 39

85

·

LIU YUNG

Yü hu tieh

Over there the rain has stopped, the sky is clearing
I lean against the rail . . . softly, softly
My eyes see off autumn's splendor
The late scene, lonely, sparse
Would move Sung Yü to grief
In rain and gentle wind, apple blossoms gradually faded
Under the moon, in cold dew, wu-t'ung leaves yellow and fly—
Enough melancholy!
Where are my friends?
There, where mist and water meet, far, too far . . .

I can't forget
The times we met to write and drink—
How many lonely poems of wind and moon since then?
How often have the stars turned, the frosts come?
The sea is vast, the mountains so far away
No way to even find the Hsiao and Hsiang—
What good then, the swallows
For sending messages?
There, in the dusk
A boat is going back—but what's the use?
I watch it gloomily—
A wild swan, lost, cries out
I linger, the glow, oblique, near spent

CST 40

Pa sheng Kan chou

Spattering evening rain sprinkles river and sky
Washes clear autumn
Soon frost with icy winds will close in
On the desolate mountain pass, the deserted river . . .
Last rays of sun glance off the tower
Everywhere red fades, green disappears
By turns, what flourished, ends
Only the waters of the Yangtze flow on
Wordlessly, east

I can not bear to climb the high tower, look out
Gaze longingly toward home—dim and distant
But to stop my thoughts from going back is hard
I wonder at my path in recent years—
Why have I lingered, miserable
Aware that in her room she has looked up—
How many times—and thought she saw my boat on the horizon?
And never known that I lean here
Congealed with sorrow?

CST 43

87
.

LIU YUNG

Chu ma tzu

Alone I climb the cold deserted fort
To a watchtower with a vast view—
Softly descending toward the misted shore
The shadow of a rainbow hangs rain
A harsh wind
Caresses the ledge
Slyly takes back what's left of summer warmth
Bit by bit—startled by a leaf, I feel autumn
Listen to the last lingering cicadas—
The seasons turn, sounds change key
The look of it brings back past pleasures
There, at the capital, beyond fog and mist, secluded places . . .

Off that way lie memories, melancholy
New sorrows gather easily
Old loves do not
All day, high up, I lean and look out
As the wind rises, my spirits droop, no one to talk to
A clear view, thin mist
Here and there scattered crows
A lonely silence settles on river and wall at dusk
An ornate cornice of the south tower
Sees off the dallying rays of sun

CST 43

LIU YUNG

Mi shen yin

My skiff with billowing sail
Moored a moment on the south bank of the Ch'u
I hear the evening horn from the desolate ramparts
Tartar flutes answer dolefully
Along the vague vast river—
On the flats, geese
Startled, fly off
Mists dissolve, a chill penetrates the wood
As on a painting
At the horizon, distant mountains look small—
Black eyebrows, sketched

Lovers once, rashly I threw her off
To come here, a wandering official
The road is bitter
Late in the year
In an alien landscape
I bear the lonely desolation
Face sorrow while my eyes
Seek in the distance for the capital
The Ch'in tower blocks the view
Sends my restless soul into confusion
Where the fragrant grasses join the void
The setting sun is full
About her, I know nothing
Our affair cut off—far away

Ch'ing pei

A flock of ducks settles, frosts the sand bar
Lines of wild geese cross the misty bank
The clear bright look of autumn, freshly painted
After a sudden evening shower
Boat moored for the night
I lodge at the inn of a mountain village—
Who, by moonlight, draws near this windy spot
And on a Tartar flute begins a thread of melody
That ravels ten thousand threads of parting sorrow?
From the grassy shore
Crickets crick—they sound like weavers

After we parted, I tried to recall her face—
Rivers and mountains away—
How could we count on fish and birds to be our messengers?
I long for her hidden chamber
She, to know of this haggard ruined
Wanderer at heaven's edge
The clouds at Ch'u gorge have dispersed
The lovers of Kao-yang gone
Only the silent lonely footprints of a madman left
To look back toward the capital—
Useless! My gaze is blocked:
Remote mountains—impasto green

CST 51

LIU YUNG

Li t'ing yen

Rivers and mountains displayed like a painting
Of an elegant autumn scene
Water soaks the sky at the horizon
Clear colors reflect cold light
Islets of smartweed, islets of flowering reeds
Bamboo and house shade one another

The traveler's sail hangs from the clouds
Beyond the smoke, the wine banner trails low
How much of moment in the Six Dynasties has history discarded?
Things end as gossip for fishermen and woodcutters
As I gaze sadly from the storied tower
A cold sun sets in the west without comment

CST 111 •

92
•

Ts'ai sang tzu

All fragrance past, still West Lake is fine
Scattered remnants of red
A drizzle of catkins
Strands of willow by the fence, all day blowing

The music of the sheng finished, the traveler gone
Spring suddenly seems spent
I lower the curtained window
Swallows in pairs return through misty rain

CST 121

94

T'a so hsing

The plum by the inn, nearly bare
Strands of willows by the bridge still slim—
With a flick of the reins, in a warm breeze, fragrant grass
The sorrow of parting spreads, extends
Vast, unbroken, like spring floods

Bit by bit
She is all powder, tears
Afraid to climb the tower, lean against the rail
Beyond the plain are mountains in full spring
But he has gone even beyond the mountains, beyond spring!

CST 123

95
·

OU-YANG HSIU

Su chung ch'ing

Clear dawn, light frost rolls with the bamboo shade
Breathing on her hands, she tries plum flower make-up
And thinks of love and parting
So, paints her brows in form of distant mountains

Remembering what's past
She grudges its passing
Now grieved
She must compose her face before she sings
Striving to smile, she frowns
It breaks one's heart

CST 123

96
·

Sheng ch'a tzu

Last year the night of the first full moon—
Flower-market lanterns bright as day—
The moon climbed high into the willow
    As after dark, we met

  This year, night and time the same
    Moon and lanterns are as bright
      But where is last year's you?
  Tears stain spring, wet my sleeve

CST 124

97
·

OU-YANG HSIU

Yü chia ao

Beneath the flowers, suddenly a swish of oars
And in a flash more girls come
Quickly lotus leaves are twisted into wine cups
On rolling lotus boats
Time and again, red waves well in the cups

Clear scent of flowers mixes with the wine's bouquet
A red cheeked flower faces a wine flushed cheek
Then in green shade we sleep it off
Startled to get up and find
The boat beached on the sand

CST 129

98
.

Yü lou ch'un

Once you left, how could I know how far you were?
　　All I could see was chill shades of melancholy
　　As, by degrees, you went endlessly, on and on
Over waters so vast, even fish sink—who knows where?

Late at night the wind through the bamboo plays autumn music
　　Ten thousand leaves, one thousand sounds—all of regret
　　　　I try to sleep, to find you in a dream
But dreams elude me still, and lamplight smolders to ash

CST 133

Nan ko tzu

Phoenix hair tied with a glittering ribbon
Jade comb with dragon tracery
She smiles, comes to me by the window
Asks lovingly—"Are my eyes done right?"

Leaning against me, she lingers, plays with my brush
Then, sketching flowers before she starts
Soon stops embroidering again
To ask, giggling, how to write "drake" and "duck"

CST 140

Lang t'ao sha

A toast to the east wind
Who, for the moment, lingers
Where willows hang along the lilac path east of Loyang
That place where hand in hand
We sauntered through fragrant groves

Together, and parted so so quickly
Unending sorrow—
This year the flowers outdo last year's red
Alas, next year's may be still better
Who knows with whom?

CST 141

101

·

OU-YANG HSIU

Ch'ing yü an

Of all the things that bloom in just one spring
Two thirds are finished
Dark green and lovely red all in confusion!
With green willows in the court
Warm breezes through the screen
A man can waste away

Buying a flower—like wine—in the Ch'ang-an market!
Can that match peach and plum in bloom?
No wonder the east wind stirs an exile's tears
This longing defies words
The you of dreams—not good enough—
If only I were home!

CST 161 *(DISPUTED)

OU-YANG HSIU

Tieh lien hua

Who says you can shake it off?
Each time, come spring
The same regrets
Days pass drunk among flowers
No escape—look at the worn face in the glass

Fresh green along the river, willows by the dyke
I ask of each new sorrow
Why it's like this, year after year
When I stand alone on the small bridge, sleeves blowing
In a quiet grove, under a new moon, and you've gone

CST 162

103

OU-YANG HSIU

Tieh lien hua

Several days moving clouds—where have you gone
Forgetting to return?
Don't tell me spring's about to end
A hundred grasses, a thousand flowers strew the way to Cold Hearth Festival
By whose house does your carriage wait?

Often, alone in the tower, eyes fill with tears, I talk to myself
When swallows come in pairs
I wonder will we meet along the lane
Disorderly sorrow drifts like catkins
I linger in dreams, but can not find you

CST 162

OU-YANG HSIU

Tieh lien hua

How deep, deep, deep the court
Willow piled on willow through the mist
Curtains and screens beyond count
Jade bit, carved saddle dally by the pleasure house
From her high tower, that road cannot be seen

Raging rain, wild April winds
Doors close on yellow dusk
Nothing will make spring stay
Tears beg the flowers, the flowers, without a word
Whirl in red chaos past the garden swing

CST 162

·

OU-YANG HSIU

Juan lang kuei

In south garden mid-spring, fresh green to walk on
A gentle breeze, the sound of horses neighing
Green plums the size of peas, catkins like eyebrows
A long day, butterflies

Dew heavy on the flowers
Mist low on the grass
At home, shades lowered
Weary from swinging, she undoes the silk clothes
In the painted hall, a pair of swallows fly

CST 162

OU-YANG HSIU

紹聖元年三月作　東坡居士

Shui lung yin

Following the rhyme of Chang Chih-fu's Willow Flower tz'u

Like a flower, but not a flower
No one cares when it falls
And lies discarded at the roadside
But, though
Unmoved, I think about
The tangle of wounded tendrils
Lovely eyes full of sleep
About to open, yet
Still in dreams, following the wind ten thousand miles
In search of love
Startled, time and again, by the oriole's cry

Do not pity the flower that flies off
Grieve for the western garden
Its fallen red already beyond mending—
Now, after morning rain
What's left?
A pond full of broken duckweed
Of the three parts of spring
Two turn to dust
One to flowing water
Look—
These are not catkins
But drop after drop of parted lovers' tears

Shui tiao ko t'ou

Mid-Autumn Festival, the year ping ch'en (1076). I gaily drink
until dawn and, completely drunk, write this, thinking of Tzu-yu.

The moon—how old is it?
I hold the cup and ask the clear blue sky
But I don't know, in palaces up there
When is tonight?
If only I could ride the wind and see—
But no, jade towers
So high up, might be too cold
For dancing with my shadow—
How could *there*, be like *here*?

Turning in the red chamber
Beneath the carved window
The brightness baffles sleep
But why complain?
The moon is always full at parting
A man knows grief and joy, separation and reunion
The moon, clouds and fair skies, waxing and waning—
An old story, this struggle for perfection!
Here's to long life
This loveliness we share even a thousand miles apart!

CST 280

Drinking Alone Under the Moon

Flowers and a jug of wine
I drink alone, since no one's here
I raise my cup, invite the moon
And with my shadow, we are three
The moon's no drinker
My shadow follows, senselessly
But for the nonce, I take the moon
To keep the shadow company!
Enjoying life, we capture spring
I sing—the moon sways to my song
I dance—my shadow tumbles in a heap
Still conscious, we enjoy each other
Drunk, we go our ways
But we were joined forever when we lost ourselves
And have a date to meet again among the stars

LI PO (701–762)

SU SHIH

Nien nu chiao

Mid-Autumn

From this high place I have a boundless view
Vast emptiness, ten thousand miles of it
Without a trace of cloud
Among the darting moonbeams
Cold soaks the whole sky autumn blue—
Jade heavens, a jasper tower—
Astride a phoenix, I come and go
From that clear cool place
Rivers and mountains spread as on a painting
In which, through mist, I see each tree

Once drunk, I clap my hands, wildly sing
Raise the cup, invite the moon
And with my shadow we are three
Let's dance in the wind and dew
This night is like no other
We'll ride back on the wind
Let's go!
Who needs a roc's wing?
From the crystal palace
The sound of a flute comes haltingly

CST 330 *

At Red Cliff, musing about ancient times

The Yangtze flows east
Washing away
A thousand ages of great men
West of the ramparts—
People say—
Are the fabled Red Cliffs of young Chou of the Three Kingdoms
Rebellious rocks pierce the sky
Frightening waves rip the bank
The backwash churns vast snowy swells—
River and mountains like a painting
How many heroes passed them, once . . .

Think back to those years, Chou Yü—
Just married to the younger Ch'iao—
Brave, brilliant
With plumed fan, silk kerchief
Laughed and talked
While masts and oars vanished to flying ash and smoke!
I roam through ancient realms
Absurdly moved
Turn gray too soon—
A man's life passes like a dream—
Pour out a cup then, to the river, and the moon

CST 282 *

·

SU SHIH

Hsi chiang yüeh

Traveling on a spring night along the Ch'i River in Huang-chou, I passed a wine shop and stopped to drink. Drunk, I followed the moon to a bridge spanning a small brook. There, I unsaddled the horse and, with my arm for a pillow, lay down to rest a little. When I awoke, it was already dawn, mountains crowding each other, the flowing river clanging against the bridge. Feeling strangely I had left the human world, I wrote this on a piling.

The overflow spills deflected moonbeams through the wilds
Across the plain, elusive veils of mist
My splendid horse still in his saddle mat
I want to sleep, drunk, in the fragrant grass

How vulnerable, a flawless brook with its seductions
Don't let the least tread shatter the jade surface
Undo the saddle, I'll sleep under green willows by the bridge
And wait for the cuckoo to announce the dawn

CST 284

Lin chiang hsien

Last night at East Slope I was drunk, sober, and drunk again—
Came back near the third watch—
The houseboy's snores already thundered
I knocked and knocked—to no effect
So rested on a stick, listening to the river

I hate it! I'm not my own person—
When will I stop this frenzied buzzing?
This late, the wind is still, the river silken—
I could take a skiff and drift
My life away, downstream, out to sea

CST 287

·

SU SHIH

Shao nien yu

Written in Jun-chou

Last year I saw you off
Outside the Yü-hang gate
Snow flew like catkins
This year's spring spent
Catkins fly like snow
You're still not back

When there's wine, I raise the shade, invite the moon—
Only wind and dew penetrate the screen—
The moon prefers a pair of swallows, nesting
Its clear bright beams
Rest on their painted eaves

CST 288

Ting feng po

On the way to Sa Lake on the seventh day of the third moon, we were caught without rain gear in a sudden shower. My companions were completely put out, but I paid no attention. Later, the sun came out and I wrote this.

Ignore it! So it penetrates the grove, beats on the leaves
Why don't we hum, whistle, take a stroll?
Bamboo staff and grass shoes are light—leave the horses
Why fret?
A straw coat will do for the mist and rain of a lifetime

Harsh spring gusts rouse me from wine—
A chill—
But see? A ray of sunshine beckons from the mountain peaks
I turn to where I'd just heard wind and rain
If I went back
There'd be no rain, no wind—but no sun either!

CST 288

·

SU SHIH

Ting feng po

Sing of the red flowering plum

Sleeping soundly, too lazy to open—don't be mad they're late
They're sorry for themselves—their pallor doesn't suit the season
Once in a while they manage a bit of red like peach or almond
But their style—
Aloof, the lingering beauty of snow and frost

What if you're not like the rest
Who cares?
New wine can color the palest cheek
Old poems miss the essence of the plum
Sing—
And it changes—look: green leaves, green branches

CST 289

SU SHIH

Wang chiang nan

Written on Ch'ao-jan Terrace

Spring just begun
The breezes blow the willows this way and that
I climb Ch'ao-jan Terrace for the view
Spring floods half fill the moat, the city, a mass of flowers
Steaming rain darkens a thousand households

Cold Hearth Festival over
Head clearing after wine, I sigh and sigh—
Why brood about old friends and home?
Better use new fire to brew new tea
Write poems, drink, and take my chances while there's time

CST 295

SU SHIH

Pu suan tzu

Written when I lived at Ting Hui Temple in Huang-chou

A fragment moon hangs from the bare t'ung tree
The water clock runs out, all is still
Who sees the dim figure come and go alone
Misty, indistinct, the shadow of a lone wild goose?

Startled, she gets up, looks back
With longing no one sees
And will not settle on any of the cold branches
Along the chill and lonely beach

CST 295 *

Ho hsin lang

Fledgling swallows fly—the splendid house
Is still, deserted
The shade of the locust turns at noon—
By evening, cool, just bathed
She toys with a round white raw silk fan—
Hand, fan, one smooth piece of jade—
And wearily lies down
Alone in deep clear sleep . . .
Who comes? Who pushes the embroidered door
For nothing
Breaks her dreams of love?
Again
Only the wind rattles the bamboo curtain

Pomegranate blossoms only half burst, red ruffled silk
And wait until more fickle flowers'
Pistils finish waving
To have you to themselves
Look carefully at this lush branch
Fragrant petals in a thousand layers
Trembling
Lest the west wind leave it green
Before you come!
Looking at that flower
She dare not touch wine
Petals and powder tears mix
Whispering as they fall

CST 297

SU SHIH

Chiang ch'eng tzu

I think of Chu K'ang-shu during a heavy snowfall.
I know he is thinking of me; so, I write this to send him.

Last evening it was just a light drizzle
This morning, the shades open
To snow almost level with the roof
The river wide, sky low
Gone, the green drapery we knew
Alone, here, cold—who will sing with me?
I rub a rheumy eye . . .
Twist a fading beard

If I were there we'd drink away this gloom
Make the salt crystal
Sweet
Hold a spray of plum blossoms
Gaze east, recalling T'ao Ch'ien
Snow is like an old friend, an old friend, like snow
However wonderful
Some will find fault

CST 299

SU SHIH

Chiang ch'eng tzu

Hunting Song

Why shouldn't an old man sprout mad youth
Pull a yellow dog with one hand
Hold a falcon in the other—
In a silk hat and sable coat
Lead a thousand horsemen over the plains?
To reward his followers, the governor
Will shoot the tiger himself
Like Sun Ch'üan

Wine bolsters courage
So my hair is slightly frosty
So what!
I'm still in charge of Yün-chung
When will the emperor send Feng T'ang
So I can stretch my bow into a full moon
Gaze north
And shoot the Sky Wolf?

cst 299

122

·

Chiang ch'eng tzu

On the twentieth day of the first moon, 1075, I record the night's dream.

Ten years living and dead have drawn apart
I do nothing to remember
But I can not forget
Your lonely grave a thousand miles away . . .
Nowhere can I talk of my sorrow—
Even if we met, how would you know me
My face full of dust
My hair like snow?

In the dark of night, a dream: suddenly, I am home
You by the window
Doing your hair
I look at you and can not speak
Your face is streaked by endless tears
Year after year must they break my heart
These moonlit nights?
That low pine grave?

CST 300

Tieh lien hua

A scattering of faded red bares apricots, small and green
Time young swallows learned to fly
Spring floods surround the house
Catkins from the willows' upper branches blow and dwindle
From here to heaven fragrant grasses grow

Inside the wall, a swing; outside, a road
Outside, a man, walking
Inside, a girl, laughing
The laughter dies away, and all is still
All but desire, fired by indifference

CST 300

Yung yü yüeh

*I lodge for the night at Swallow Pavilion,
dream of P'an P'an, and write this tz'u.*

Moonlight like frost
A fine breeze along the water
The view clear and limitless
In the inlet, fish jump
Round lotus leaves drip dew
In the solitary stillness
Of the third watch—
A leaf shatters on the ground
Breaks my erotic dream—
In the vast night
I can not find her again
Awake, alone, I walk in the small garden

I have traveled to the borders of heaven
Mountains block my return
Eye and heart strain toward home until they break
Swallow Tower is empty
What has become of its lovely lady?
Now only swallows are locked in
The past is like a dream
When one wakes
Pleasure fades, regret lingers . . .
You who will come
To my Yellow Tower on such a night
Sigh for me

125

•

CST 302

SU SHIH

Yang kuan ko

Written on Mid-Autumn Festival

The evening clouds disappear, it's clear and cold
The river of stars turns about the full moon
Life on this night is not often good
Next year's moon—from where will we see it?

CST 311

·

Huan ch'i sha

*Sauntering about the Temple of Clear Spring on the Ch'i
River—the temple looks out on Orchid River which flows West.*

At the foot of the hill, small orchid shoots wade in the river
The dirt road through the pines is dry
Through the whispering evening rain, a nightjar calls

Who says one can't be young again
If even the river by the door flows west?
Don't rush white hair helping the yellow cock to crow!

CST 314

Drinking Song

Who says you don't appreciate music
Listen to the yellow cock, watch the white sun
The yellow cock rushes the morning crowing too early
The white sun rushes the years as they pass
The red sash of office barely tied
Youth's blush in the mirror, already lost . . .

PO CHÜ-I (772–846)

SU SHIH

Huan ch'i sha

Giving thanks for rain along the road at Stone
Lake in Hsü-men, I wrote these five pieces.

I

Fish flash in reflected sunlight, red, warm
While in the village dark green evening already hides the birds
Golden children, white old men, gather happily

Deer wander through the crowd, surprised
Monkeys, at the first sound of drums, begin to shriek—
Go tell the girls out picking mulberries to come!

II

In a whirl they rouge, dress, fly to gape at the Imperial Envoy
Flock about the bramble gates
Pushing and shoving until red skirts are torn

Old, young, propped up, led, attend the sacrifice
Wheeling crows vie for the village offering
By evening, drunk old men sleep beside the road

III

Hemp leaves piled layer on bright layer—
Which house cooks cocoons? The whole village is fragrant
Soft voiced girls chat over fences as they reel silk

Old men with sticks look about, bleary drunk
With green wheat buns in their hungry stomachs
They wonder when the bean leaf will be ripe

IV

Falling date blossoms whisper against my clothes
South of the village and north, the sounds of reeling silk
A rough clad farmer sells squash by the old willow

Wine-tired on the long road, I only wanted sleep
Now the sun is high, I long for tea
And knock on a country door to ask for some

SU SHIH

V

Soft grass, flat clover, fresh just after rain
The horses on fine sand raise no dust
When will I work things out, go back to farm?

Warm sun splashes off mulberry and hemp
The wind carries the fragrance of herbs—
Once, I was part of all this

CST 316

Huan ch'i sha

*1084, the twenty-fourth day of the twelfth moon. I go
with Liu Ching-shu to Suchou to enjoy South Mountain.*

Fine rain and wind have left a chill
Clear skies, seductive willows cloaked in mist, scattered along the banks
The clear Lo empties into the Huai

White bubbles, the floating flowers of noon tea
Luxuriant shoots and sprouts in a spring dish
All this to savor—what pure delight!

CST 318 *

134

.

SU SHIH

Ch'ing yü an

*I follow Ho Fang-hui's rhyme in a farewell
to Po-ku on his return home to Wu-chung.*

Three years I've dreamed of the road back to Wu-chung
I'll send Yellow Ears
With you—
In case you pass Sung-chiang, call the small ferry—
The gulls, the egrets—don't startle them
The place where the four bridges are, Lao Tzu once walked

The painting of Wang-ch'uan in late spring
Recalls lines of the great minister's verse
Heaven has set the day for your return
My spring clothes—
Still Hsiao Man's work—
Are wet with West Lake rain

CST 320

Man t'ing fang

Written on a summer day on No-thought Hill in Li Shui

Wind has matured the infant oriole
Rain fattened plums
At noon the shade of trees is true and round
On low ground near the hills
Damp clothes need incense smoke to dry
Quietly, I watch birds frolic
Beyond the little bridge, new green splashes
I linger against the rail—
Yellow reeds, bitter bamboo—
If only I could drift in the boat at Chiu-chiang . . .

Year in year out
Migrating like the swallow
Back and forth over the vast desert
Lodging on long rafters—
Why look beyond the moment?
I'll keep close to the wine
Wretched and spent, a stranger from the south
I hate the sound of the fast pipes and jumbled strings
Wide of the feast
I'll spread my mat and pillow
Then I can sleep, when drunk

CST 601

138

Kuo ch'in lou

Bathing in the water, a clear moon
Crackling leaves, a breath of cool
Along the lane, the clatter of horses dies away
Idling by the well
I laughed to see her chase a stream of fireflies
And tear the patterned silk of her fan . . .
Through long quiet nights, leaning by the rail
Too troubled to sleep
I stand until the hands of the clock have nearly finished out the night
The good years passed in a flash
Now she's a thousand miles away
Beyond dreams, too far for letters

What's the use of saying my hair fears the jade comb—
My face so drawn in the mirror—
I've grown too lazy to fix or color it
The breeze in the plums, earthy, steaming
Sprinkled by the rainbow, mosses riot
The trellis is alive with dancing red, just turned
Who would believe I feel this way because of her?
Chiang Yen's skill is gone
My grief, that of Hsün Ch'ing
Only in the shadow of the Milky Way
Can I still pinpoint the occasional star

CST 602

139

CHOU PANG-YEN

Su mu che

Burning garu wood
Dispels the summer dampness
Birds greet clear skies
Chattering and peeping about the eaves at dawn
Early sun dries last night's rain from leaves
Floating in clear rounds on the water
The lotus, one by one, nod to the wind

I don't belong here—
When can I go
Back to Wu-men?
I have stayed on in the capital so long
Would May fishermen even remember me
If a small oar and a light boat
Took me in dreams, back to the lotus pond?

CST 603

CHOU PANG-YEN

Yeh yu kung

Falling leaves, the sunset on the river
Rippling for a thousand miles
On the bridge, harsh winds pierce my eyes
I linger
Day fades
Lamps are lit along the streets

In the cold under my window in the old house
I hear each leaf that falls from the wu-t'ung by the well
My quilt won't hold me, alone, I can't stay still—
She knows
That for her
I write this

CHOU PANG-YEN

Chieh yü hua

Lantern Festival

Candles flare and melt in the wind
Staining the paper lotus with red dew
In the streets lanterns dazzle one another
Moonlight cascades over tiled roofs
Light clouds scatter
The bright moon goddess longs to join
Lovely girls in light dresses
Their waists slender as those of Ch'u—
Flutes and drums clamor for attention
Peoples' shadows blend in disarray
A drifting fragrance fills the air

It brings back nights at the capital, when, curfew waived
Lights on a thousand gates turned night to day—
I reveled in the carnival—
The wave of a silk handkerchief from a gilded carriage
And where we met
Horses kicked up dark dust . . .
This year's festival is as bright
Only the thrill has gone
In time's wake
Coaches, calash flying, come again—
Let them pass, let the dance end, for me the songs are over

CST 608 *

142

CHOU PANG-YEN

Liu ch'ou

Written after the roses faded

Time to wear light clothes again, taste wine
How I regret the days and nights I've thrown away!
If only spring had stayed a little
And not brushed past
Now suddenly there's nothing left
Ask where the flowers are
Last night brought wind and rain . . .
Those whose beauty toppled kings are buried with Ch'u Palace
But where each filigree hairpin fell there is a fragrant remnant—
Disheveling the peach path
Fluttering along a lane of willows . . .
I loved too well—who now will feel for me?
Only matchmaking bees and butterfly messengers
That knock from time to time at the window

The east garden is quiet
Gradually thick with green
That stealthily coiled beneath prized sprays
I sigh for
A long shoot catches as I pass
Pulls at my clothes as if about to speak
A sense of loss that is infinite
Over a faded flower that is nothing!
Better pin it to my turban
Where it will no longer seem

143

.

A blossom trembling in your hair
As it leans toward me
Petals drift everywhere—oh, do not drift off with the tides—
Your broken red may still have words of love
For me to see

cst 610 *

Chou Pang-Yen

Lan ling wang

Willows

A row of willows neatly shades the bank
Strand by strand they green the mist
Along the Sui dykes
I know them all already
Branches trailing the water, catkins blowing—hue and cast of partings
When I came, I climbed the hills to gaze toward home
Who knows
What it is to be a weary stranger in the capital
On the road of post stations
Year in, year out?
The willow strands I've broken, end to end, would reach a thousand feet

Had I time, I'd search for traces of the past
But once again, wine and sad music speed me on
Lanterns light the farewell dinner
Pear blossoms and elm fires press to spring festivals
I hate the wind that carries me faster
As the boat poles the warm waves . . .
Several stations race by before I turn
And see you at the edge of heaven

Chill misery
Grief piled on grief
Gradually, the churning of the water where we parted
At the pier grows quiet

Reluctantly, the sun sets on a boundless spring
I remember how we held hands by moonlit pavilions
And listened to a flute at a dew covered bridge
Lost in the past
Now like a dream
My tears fall stealthily

CST 611

CHOU PANG-YEN

Hsi ho

Nanking

A splendid sight, still
But who remembers its glory in the Six Dynasties?
Mountains surround the Old Kingdom, a clear river binds
Hills that rise like the piled hair of lovely girls
The angry surf beats at the city wall
High masts, in the wind, trace the horizon

A tree clings to the jagged cliff
Still hanging on, aslant
Mo Ch'ou once tied her boat there—
Useless now, a relic, thick with green
Fog presses on the ruins
Deep in the night, the moon vaults the battlements
How painful to gaze east toward the Huai!

What has become of the wine shop banners, the theater drums?
Here, I think, were once the Wang and Hsieh estates
Now, baffled swallows that frequented those halls
Find the lanes of common folk
And chatter one to another as of men's rise and fall
In the sunset

CST 612

147
.

CHOU PANG-YEN

Wu Yi Lane

Weeds and wild flowers beside the Chu-ch'üeh bridge
Shafts of the setting sun enter Wu Yi Lane
Homing swallows that once graced mansions of the Wangs and Hsiehs
Still seek them, but fly into a hundred humble homes

Nanking

Mountains surround the Old Kingdom
The surf beats at the desolate city, sadly withdraws
East of the Huai, the moon of former times
Deep in the night still vaults the battlements

LIU YÜ-HSI (772–842)

CHOU PANG-YEN

P'u sa man

Plum Blossoms in the Snow

The silver river traces out three thousand bends
Wild ducks bathe in it, cranes fly above the pure green waves
But where's the boat bringing him back—
Evening glows at those houses on the shore . . .

Heaven, jealous of rioting plum blossoms
Covers the branches with snow
But she, in the inner court, shade rolled, gazing out—
She's meant to pity them, freezing by the water!

CST 612

CHOU PANG-YEN

Tieh lien hua

A moon so bright the crows are restless
The night is ending
Someone draws water from the well
I wake you—two bright eyes
Shed tears that blossom on the pillow, cold and red

Hands touch, a frosty wind blows the shadow of your hair
Loath to go
Our words of parting pain my ear
Above the stairs, the handle of the Dipper passes the rail
Out in cold dew, far away, I hear cocks call, and call

CST 614

Yü mei jen

Fences of small farms scattered along the winding path
Mist, trees taking shape—dawn
In the cold, mountain peaks float as if on nothing
At the first bell, from the wilderness, a lone skiff sets sail

I bundle up, urge the horse on to find a post station
Only wine will ease my sorrow
Ducks asleep in the rushes of a pond by the slope
Startled by my passing, fly up, only to find each other again

CST 618

Tsui lo p'o

Going to look at Ching-lung Gate on the eve of
Lantern Festival: a lament for Queen Ming Chieh

Words catch in my throat—
The lanterns bring back this day other years—
Strolling here, there, pointing to the moon, on and on, talking
We wanted the moon full forever
Not so quickly dented

This year, flower lanterns displayed in rows
Beautiful as before, but oh how different!
To this lady, here, I can't explain
I dare not raise my head
Ashamed to see the moon of former times

CST 897

CHAO CHI (EMPEROR HUI-TSUNG)

Lin chiang hsien

Winter, 1125. On the way to Po-chou with the imperial entourage

Across rivers, through mountains, we press on
Chanting verses—a thousand odd lines
Intense cold, the Huai rough in sparse rain
Mist blankets the herons on the shoal
I buy the last of the day's catch from a boat

A dismal old temple is all there is
For the night—a monk's cell
My soul escapes in dreams, and yet . . .
Sorrow hangs on my heart
Blends with tears as I answer your letter

CST 897

155
·

CHAO CHI (EMPEROR HUI-TSUNG)

T'an ch'un ling

Shades and banners rippling
In piercing cold
The ice on Dragon Pond has melted
Almond blossoms scoff, their scent elusive still
And yet
Spring's near half done

Clear song and subtle dances can't begin
Until the air is fragrant, and we start the feast
Remember last year?
In the spring breeze?
We vowed that neither oriole nor flower would be wasted

CST 897

CHAO CHI (EMPEROR HUI-TSUNG)

Yen shan t'ing

Tailored white silk
Lightly folded, layers
Delicately rouged
The latest thing in lovely make-up
Beauty and fragrance extravagantly blended—
Perfection that puts girls in heaven's palaces to shame
Not only quick to fade
But prey to the brutal wind and rain—
I grieve for
The abandoned garden—they fall, and leave it desolate
How many springs have I watched end here?

The miseries of exile pile up one by one
My only messengers, a brace of swallows
Who can not speak
The sky is endless, earth vast
Ten thousand rivers, a thousand mountains
Where is there word of what was once my palace?
Not brood? How?
Only in dreams have I been back—
That's nothing to rely on—
Lately I can't even do that

CST 898

157

•

CHAO CHI (EMPEROR HUI-TSUNG)

Ju meng ling

Remember that night by the river pavilion
When, too drunk to find our way
The party over, we tried to row back
And tangled with lotus in deep water somehow?

Struggling to cross
Struggling to cross
We suddenly flushed a shoalful of birds

CST 927

160
.

Ju meng ling

Last night showers and harsh winds—
Despite thick sleep, wine lingers—
I worry the girl raising the shades
"No, no," she says, "the crab apple's just as it was"

Doesn't she know?
Doesn't she know?
The green ought to be fat, the red, thin

CST 927

Yü chia ao

Sky, milky way and morning mist blend
In the River of Stars, a thousand sails dance
As in a dream, my soul returns to heavenly palaces—
I hear the gods
Ask eagerly where I go

The way is long, I sigh, the day late
What good to study poetry, write striking lines?
In ninety thousand li of wind, the roc just flies
Wind, do not stop
Blow the grass boat to the three mountains

CST 927

Yi chien mei

Fragrance—red lotus—lingers, though the mat had the feel of autumn
I loosen my clothes,
Boarding the skiff alone . . .
Whose silk letter will come from the clouds
When the geese return in formation
And the moon is full by the west chamber?

Petals drift off, the river flows
A single longing
Darkens two places
I can't escape it
When it falls from my brow
It rises to my heart

CST 928

163

LI CH'ING-CHAO

Feng huang t'ai shang yi ch'ui hsiao

Parting

Incense cools in the gold lion
My quilt is tossed into a red sea
I get up, carelessly do my hair
Let make-up gather dust in its case
The sun's already to the curtain hook
I dread it—parting, and the anguish, after . . .
How many things I want to say—and don't
Now I'll grow thin again
Not from wine
Not from autumn melancholy

No! No!
Don't go this time
I'll sing Yang-kuan ten thousand times
To keep you
When you went as far as Wu-ling
Mist enclosed my tower here in Ch'in
And only the river passed
Take pity on me—always watching, waiting
Eyes fixed on a far place
Doomed now again to measure, day by day, a new length of sorrow

CST 928

LI CH'ING-CHAO

Huan ch'i sha

Idly looking out at spring aging in the yard
Through screens not yet closed against the gathering shadows
Up where I lean is silence: I tune the ch'in

Far off, mountains rising from mountains hasten dusk
A slim wind blows the rain, trifles with fickle darkness
The blossoming pear can't wait to fade—how can I stop it?

CST 928

Tsui hua yin

A fine mist, dense clouds—the whole long dreary day
Incense smolders in the golden beast—
Another Double Ninth—
On the pillow, under the gauze net
I wait for the first trace of midnight cool to penetrate

After we drank at dusk by the eastern fence
Our sleeves were filled with elusive fragrance
Don't say it is not affecting
To see the shade, rolled by the west wind
And feel more fragile than those yellow flowers

CST 929

LI CH'ING-CHAO

T'ien tzu ts'ai sang tzu

Already the banana palm we planted by the window
Shades the whole yard
Shades the whole yard
Leaf by leaf, cluster by cluster
Spreading, furling—overwrought

The echo of the third watch rain in the afflicted heart
Clear drop by drop
Cold drop by drop
Resonates—anguish—separation
I can't get used to it!

CST 930 *

Nien nu chiao

Spring Turbulence

Chilling both house and yard
Again a driving wind, fine rain
The doors ought to be closed—
Willows and flowers profit, as the Day of Cold Meals nears—
This sort of weather vexes only people . . .
The poem of impossible rhymes is finished
Head clearing, as after wine
I taste a special sort of idleness
The geese have passed
I'm left ten thousand thoughts, unsent

Upstairs for several days, spring cold
Curtains shield all sides
Carelessly I lean against the balustrade—
Quilt wanting, fragrance gone, new dreams
Have forced this troubled person to get up
Clear dew of morning flows
Sprouting wu-t'ung trees are suddenly inviting
How many ways spring tempts me out!
The sun is high, mists shrink—
I look again—will it clear at last, or not yet?

CST 931

LI CH'ING-CHAO

Yung yü yüeh

The sun's gold melts over the horizon
Evening clouds form strings of white jade
Where is he?
Dense fog taints the willows
The wind sighs through the plums . . .
How much of spring has gone!
Lantern festival
The weather: perfect
Prelude to the wind and rain to come
Friends call for me
In fragrant carts drawn by fine horses
I turn away both revelers and poets

In Chung-chou in the good days
There was no end of time behind girls' doors
To mark the date
We dressed our hair with feathers
Twisted gold, white silk, and willow sprays
Competing in our finery
Now, all is faded, faded
Hair disheveled, temples gray
Now, going out at night
Is not so good as hiding under the bamboo shade
Listening to others laugh and talk

CST 931

169

LI CH'ING-CHAO

Wu ling ch'un

The wind has dropped leaving the earth fragrant with fallen flowers
I know it's late, but what's the use of doing my hair?
Things go on, all but you—everything is finished
And all I had to say has turned to tears

Along the Shuang, I hear it's still spring—
If only I could take the skiff there!
But I'm afraid—that light boat on the Shuang—
How could it carry so much sorrow?

CST 931

LI CH'ING-CHAO

Sheng sheng man

Searching, searching, again and again
Cold and still, cold and still
Bitter bitter, cruel cruel sorrow—
Fever, chills—
No stay, no rest
Two, three cups of thin wine
Can not hold off the evening or delay the wind
The geese have passed
And left me sick at heart
Though once, we were old friends

The ground is full of yellow flowers piling up
Dry, brittle, wounded
Who can pick them now?
I keep my vigil by the window
Alone, how can I stand its getting dark?
And the wu-t'ung, and thin rain?
Dusk, day fades, bit by bit, drop by drop
One thing after another
How can one small word *grief* tell it all?

CST 932

Lin chiang hsien

Ou-yang Hsiu wrote a Tieh lien hua *with the line "Deep, deep, deep, how deep." I love it. I used the words in the line "How deep, deep, deep the court" to write several original tz'u to the tune* Lin chiang hsien.

How deep, deep, deep the court
Mists outside the window, fog beyond locked chambers
The tips of the willow, the buds on the plum coming out
Spring at home again in the trees of Mo-ling
I still a stranger within its tranquil walls

Wind, moon, how much there was to sing about!
Now, no one is left, I've nothing . . .
Who values lines of care, tracings of misery?
I've no heart to flirt at Lantern Festival
Even walking in the snow no longer tempts me

CST 929 [•]

Lin chiang hsien

The Flowering Plum

How deep, deep, deep the court
Clouds press against the window, fog seeps in—late spring—
Why is it haggard, scent and grace spoiled?
Last night, a clear good dream
There should be blossoms on the southern branches

Its jade, fragile; the ebony, cavalier—I hate it!
Don't play the ch'iang flute by the south tower
Even the fragrance might be blown away! Who could know
In warm breezes and late sun
It would be finished before the almond blooms?

CST 933

·

LI CH'ING-CHAO

Ju meng ling

Who for company in bright moonlight?
My shadow makes me two
The lamp burns out, time to sleep
Even he abandons me

What now?
What now?
I'm lost—what's left?

CST 935 * (DISPUTED)

174
•

LI CH'ING-CHAO

Tieh lien hua

Leaving Hsiao Yi

Along the path, I hear a flute—Cold Hearth Festival soon—
The rain has left the orchard
Filled with floating fragrance, shining blossoms
In a thousand li of slanting sun—with bells about to herald darkness
I lean from the look-out, strain to see far south for news

From the farthest seas to the edge of heaven
For thirty years
Nowhere was free of lingering regret
If heaven weren't indifferent I would ask
How it can bear to turn a lover gray?

CST 1585

LU YU

Ch'ai t'ou feng

Hands of a delicate tint
Pour golden wine
The city all in spring, and she, the willow behind the palace wall
An east wind, full of malice
Brought thin joy
And a skein of sorrows—
Years of separation—
Wrong, wrong, wrong

Spring still spring
It's we, without reason, waste away
Tears streak rouge, stain silks
Peach blossoms fall
Your room by the pond, empty—
What good our vows have stood like mountains?
With even letters barred—
And nothing, nothing, nothing

CST 1585

177

·

LU YU

Chi hsiang szu

At the source of the river, fine rain, light mist
The season of cold food, falling flowers
Whirling red, drifting white
Tarnished clouds, dark brocade
A swatch of sorrow

Vexed, even the sun shuns the place
Doesn't care
Abandons me to wine
How then can I stand to see
The air alive with the mad chase
Of willow down and samaras from the elm?

CST 1593

Ch'üeh ch'iao hsien

Colored lanterns where they gamble
Emblazoned saddles to gallop in the hunt
About great deeds, old times—who cares?
Carousers, one by one, get marquisates—
Not me! I'm off to the river to fish

A light eight-footer
With two small sails
Can conquer duckweed, usurp the misty shoal
Mirror Lake belongs to the idler
Who needs a king's favor?

CST 1595 *

Ch'üeh ch'iao hsien

Hearing a Cuckoo Cry in the Night

Beneath the thatch, as under eaves—all are quiet
The window, overgrown, screens lamplight
Late spring rains on the river, wind . . .
From orioles in the forest, swallows nesting, never a sound
But on a moonlit night, the cuckoo's sure to cry

Bring tears
Break off a lonely dream
And fly again to some secluded branch
Even at home, hearing it is terrible—
But with life half over, alone, in wayside inns . . .

CST 1595

Su chung ch'ing

Young, I rode ten thousand miles to earn a title—
With just a horse to guard Liang-chou—
Where did I trade my dreams of moat and castle
For the dust on an old seal coat?

The enemy's not wiped out
But my hair is gray—
No point crying—
Who'd have thought my life would pass
With heart still on Mount T'ien
And body rotting in Ts'ang-chou?

CST 1596

Hsieh ch'ih ch'un

In my prime: a soldier
Eager to swallow up the enemy
Array vast troops, raise the night beacons
Red faced, black haired
To press my lance at the western front—
Mocked by officialdom: I was out of step . . .

I awoke from dreams of glory
Adrift in a flat boat in Wu or Ch'u
Humming sad songs, lamenting the past
Mist and wave as far as I could see
What became of the Ch'in fortress?
I sigh that the passing years passed for nothing

CST 1597

·

LU YU

Mo yü erh

In 1179, I was relieved of my post as Assistant Fiscal Intendant in Hupei and sent to Hunan. At a farewell party given by my colleague, Wang Cheng-chih, at a small mountain pavilion, I wrote this.

How much more wind and rain can they withstand?
Spring's in a rush again to go
Loving it, I dread even the flowers' opening too soon
How much worse then, this shower of red past counting?
Wait spring!
I hear the fragrant grass at heaven's edge blocks the way
Faulting spring without a word
Is only the diligent spider
Who drops his web from the painted cornice
And, all day, snatches at flying catkins

Plans at Long Gate
Made to bring back halcyon days—absurd
A beauty that once was envied
Even with gold to buy a poem by Hsiang-ju—
What plea could quicken the pulse of desire now?
Oh, do not dance
Don't you see, Jade Ring and Flying Swallow have gone to dust?
Futile regrets are worst
Come away from leaning by the high rail
There, in the sun's last slant rays
Where mist and willow are, there hearts break

CST 1867

184

·

Ch'in yüan ch'un

My new house at Tai Lake is almost finished

The three paths are just done
Cranes grumble, the ape's surprised
I myself have not yet come
Intent on cloud and mountain
My whole life
I scoffed at officials
Who stayed in office until the end—
Weary of purpose, one should retire
Seek repose in time—
No, not simply for the taste of seaweed and lu fish
When autumn settles along the river
See how the geese evade the bow strings
Returning boats avoid the backwash?

At east mountain, I'll remodel the thatched hut
So all the large windows facing the water, open
I'll fish from a skiff
But first, I should plant willows
Build fences to protect bamboo
That would not block my view of plums
In autumn I could eat chrysanthemums
In spring, wear orchids
Wait with the planting, I'll do it myself—
Hmm, but I wonder . . .
What if the emperor can't spare me yet . . .
Misgivings baffle my design

185

CST 1868

HSIN CH'I-CHI

Shui lung yin

A climb to Shang-hsin Pavilion in Nanking

In Ch'u the sky spans a thousand miles of dazzling autumn
Water to the edge of heaven erases the horizon
To see those distant mountains
Compounds anger with despair
Hairpin peaks, styled high twists—
As the sun sets behind the tower
A solitary goose cries out
I, far from home here in the south
Draw a Wu sword, and, having looked at it
Tap 'round the rail—
No one would understand
This restlessness

Don't say lu fish are ready to be minced
Even if the west wind blows
Would Chang Chi-ying go home?
To beg for land, ask for a house—
I'd be ashamed to meet
Liu Lang! Ability and spirit
Wasted in the flow of years—
Worn by the wind and rain
Even trees droop
Who can be called to bring
Red handkerchief, green sleeve
To wipe these tears of baffled valor?

CST 1869

186

Man chiang hung

Traveling on the river, rhyming with Yang Chi-weng

I have seen the mountains and rivers
We're quite old friends
I still remember, and in dreams can travel everywhere
South of the river and north
Lovely places one should visit with just a staff—
The shoes I've worn out in a lifetime!
I scoff at the world's work—what a waste for thirty-nine years
Always the official, the wanderer

The lands of Wu and Ch'u
Rise to the east and south
The great deeds
Of the rivals Ts'ao and Liu
Blown away by the west wind
Left no trace
By the time the watchtower is finished, its occupant is dead
The banners not yet furled, my head white
I sigh over life's vagaries, now sad, now happy
Now, as in ancient times

CST 1870 *

Shui tiao ko t'ou

A Covenant with the Gulls

Tai Lake—how I love
Those acres of mirroring green!
Sir Straw Shoes wouldn't mind
Walking around it a thousand times a day
Since I, the gulls, and egrets all agree
From this day on
To come and go on easy terms—
But where's the white crane
Can't we try to bring him too?

I rend pale duckweed
Push aside the green water grass
Stop on dark moss
To spy on fish, laugh at their antics
And don't forget to raise my cup
To the deserted lake, desolate hills of former times
To the bright moon, clear wind of tonight
Man—what joy, what sorrow he has known!
The east bank has little green, too little shade—
I should plant more willows over there

CST 1871

188
·

HSIN CH'I-CHI

Shui tiao ko t'ou

When the boat anchors at Yangchou, I follow your rhyme

At sunset, beyond the Wall, dust rises
Hu horsemen hunt in clear autumn
A hundred thousand Chinese troops
Lined up, their feet like a storied tower
Who said to throw their whips in, and who that they should fly across?
I remember long ago the sound of arrows tinged with blood
Only wind and rain mourn Fo Li—
Su Ch'in was then still young
With just a horse and dark sable coat

Now I've grown old
I scratch white hair
Passing Yangchou
Tired of office, I want to drift on the river
Plant a thousand orange trees with my own hand
If you two seek fame in the southeast
Make ten thousand books of poems your career—
Take my advice—
Don't try to shoot the tigers of Nan Shan
Just look for money and a marquisate

CST 1873

189
·

HSIN CH'I-CHI

Nien nu chiao

Written on a wall in Tung-liu Village

Wild crab apple blossoms falling
Ch'ing-ming, too, has hurried by
For no reason the east wind cheats me of a dream
Which suddenly shies from pillow and screen turned cold
By the cove where you once held the goblet
I tie my horse to the hanging willow
Where once I lightly said good-bye
The house is empty, you gone
Errant then, I've only flying swallows to confide in now

I heard at the end of the lovely east lane
A passer-by has seen
Delicate feet behind the curtain
The old desire surges, inexhaustible as the river in spring
The new, clouds the mountains for a thousand miles
Perhaps tomorrow
We will meet again over the wine cup
The flower in the mirror is hard to pick
And I wonder—alarmed—
How gray your hair would be by now

CST 1874

190

HSIN CH'I-CHI

Che ku t'ien

Returning from O Lake sick, I got up to write this

On pillow and mat in the house by the creek, a chill—autumn coming
Broken clouds, low on the water, gathered up at evening
Flushed lotus flop, like drunks, one on the other
White birds bring no word, I resign myself to melancholy

I write in the air, alarmed, dismayed—
But let it be, let it be
A hill, a valley, it's scenery enough . . .
How weak I've grown
Lately, I can't even climb the stairs

CST 1879

Mu lan hua man

*Written at the farewell banquet for Chang Chung-ku
who has been sent to take command of Hsing-yüan*

At Han-chung the great age of the Han began
Is this the place—
·   Or not?
Think of it, sword set against the three parts of Ch'in
The king won!
The war over, he marched east again . . .
Those times are over
Now things are different—
Even if mountains and rivers look the same—enough to make one cry
The sun sets, but Hu dust never settles
The west wind blows along the Wall, horses grow strong—for what?

A book of strategy guided that emperor
A trivial command takes you west
A hasty banquet
And quickly you set off
Let sorrow fill your banners
When you think of me
Where you turn
Autumn envelops the river among the shadows of the first migrating geese
If only the wheels of your cart were square
My belt would not grow loose

CST 1881

HSIN CH'I-CHI

P'u sa man

Written about Tsao-k'ou cliffs in Kiangsi

Into the waters of the Ch'ing beneath Yü-ku look-out
How many a wanderer's tears were shed?
Look there—northwest, toward Ch'ang-an
And rue the ranges beyond count

Those green hills block but can not stop
The current—it still flows east
But on the river late at night, sorrows gather
And, deep in the mountains, you can hear partridge call

CST 1880 *

Mu lan hua man

At Ch'u-chou I see off Assistant Prefect Fan

Old age comes, feeling and taste go
We drink at parting
And fear the flowing years
Count the autumn festivals
When the full moon
Did not shine on our reunion!
The river doesn't care—
Nor the west wind—
They only speed your boat away . . .
Late autumn seaweed—lu fish along the river
Deep in the night, the lamps of children, fishing

Battle dress
Would be the thing to wear to court
Jade Palace trusted counselors
Might seek a midnight audience
Write edicts
Not discard all plans for our defense
If in Ch'ang-an old friends ask for me
Say sorrow is congealed with wine in my intestines still
I see only to the horizon, where geese fall from autumn skies
And when I'm drunk, sometimes, I vainly play the ch'in

CST 1881 *

HSIN CH'I-CHI

Chu ying t'ai chin

Late Spring

We divided the hair pin
At Peach Leaf Crossing . . .
Dark mist and willow on the south bank
I dare not climb the tower
Nine days in ten, wind and rain
The flying red breaks my heart, petal by petal
No one can prevent it—
Who could tell the chirping oriole to stop his song?

Stealthily, from my hair
I take the flower to divine the date of your return
Take it to count, again and again—
Behind the silk screen, when the lamp grows faint
I sob, even in dreams! Tell me
Is it spring that brings sorrow?
Then why, when it goes
Doesn't it take sorrow with it?

cst 1882 *

195
·

Ch'ing yü an

Lantern Festival

A night the east wind bares a thousand trees in bloom
And knows there'll be a shower of shooting stars
Fine horses draw carved carts, perfume the roads
Excited by the music of the phoenix flute
Jade lamps spin—
Fish, dragons dance all night

Lovely girls in pearls and jade, golden willow strands in their hair
Laugh, talk, seductively—a secret fragrance is missing
I look for her in the crowd a thousand times—
Suddenly, a turn of the head—
There she is in the shattered lamplight!

CST 1884

HSIN CH'I-CHI

Ho hsin lang

Taking leave of my twelfth younger brother, Mao-chia

Hear the t'i-chüeh in green trees
And worse, the che-ku's silence
And the tu-chüan sounding sharp and sad
Crying that spring is nowhere to be found
How bitter this end to fragrance
But what, compared to human partings?
Playing the p'i p'a as her horse was led beyond the Wall to darkness—
Or in a green cart, banished from the gold palace to Long Gate
Only swallows dared
See off the bride who was sent back

The general of a hundred victories, disgraced
Looked back ten thousand miles
And bade his friend farewell forever
At the Yi a cold west wind—sighed, sighed
When they gathered in white mourning like the snow
To hear the destined hero's tragic song, still incomplete
If the crying bird knew such sorrows
He'd never cry clear tears—but blood
Who now will
Drink with me under the moon?

CST 1914

Han kung ch'un

The First Day of Spring

Spring did come back
Look in her hair
A graceful spring ribbon
But for no reason, wind and rain
Refuse to make an end of the remaining cold
It's time for swallows
Perhaps tonight they'll dream of reaching the west garden—
But the wine soaked oranges aren't ready
Nor has the scallion dish been ordered

Do not smile at the east wind
Even if now it must smear the plum, dye the willow
Without a moment spare
By and by it will be back—there, in the mirror
To fade your blush
From brightness to sorrow, nonstop
Who can break the chain?
I dread anew to see the flowers bloom, the flowers fall
The geese that come at dawn will be the first to go

CST 1921

T'ai ch'ang yin

Written in Nanking on Moon Festival for Lü Shu-ch'ien

The autumn wheel, reflected, gilds the waves
The flying mirror, polishing things up again
Raising my cup, I ask the moon goddess:
What is a man to do, when white hair mocks him?

Ride the wind
Ten thousand li into the sky?
Look down on mountains, rivers?
Chop down the moon's laurel that sways in the breeze?
People say there'd be more light . . .

CST 1927

199

.

HSIN CH'I-CHI

Tien chiang ch'un

In the winter of 1187, I crossed the Wu-sung River and wrote this

Geese and swallows are stupid
They chase the clouds
Toward barren peaks
Resigned, at dusk, to rain

Beside the fourth bridge
I'd have liked to live like T'ien Sui
Instead
I just lean on the rail, think of the past
While faded willows dance in disarray

CST 2171

CHIANG K'UEI

Che ku t'ien

*Sightseeing on the eleventh day of New Year when
the lanterns are being prepared for Lantern Festival*

Now is the time to enjoy the sights along the lane
Before the torches of the rich are lit, horses neigh impatiently
A white-haired nobody needs no one to clear his path
Just a small girl on his shoulders for company

The market is ablaze with flowers
Clothes drenched in moonlight
This taste of youth in age—unsettling
At Sha-ho Creek it's not so cold in early spring . . .
I linger, put off going home

CST 2172

203

·

CHIANG K'UEI

T'a so hsing

*Coming east from Mien, I reached Chin-ling on New Year's
day 1187. On the river, moved by a dream, I wrote this.*

The grace of swallows
Enchanting as the oriole
She turns again to dreams—
How long each night, only a lover knows—
Spring from the start is tainted by desire

After I left, there were letters
Embroidery to pass the time
Bereft, her dreaming soul steals close to me, far
From Huai-nan where the white moon chills a thousand mountains
And through dark shadows, goes back, alone

CST 2174

204
·

CHIANG K'UEI

Ch'i t'ien yüeh

In 1196 Chang Kung-fu and I went to drink at Chang Ta-k'e's house.
Between the walls we could hear the crickets. Kung-fu asked each of us
to write something about them for the singer. He himself finished his
composition first—it was very beautiful. I was still pacing by the blos-
soming jasmine. When I looked up, I saw the autumn moon, which
inspired me to write this. Crickets—dubbed ts'u-chih [urge-to-weave]
in the capital—are expert fighters. Frivolous people sometimes spend
two to three hundred thousand cash for one, and then carve an ivory
tower in which to keep it.

Yü Hsin sang first "Of Sorrow"
Ch'i ch'i—I hear lovers whispering
Where dew wets the brass knocker
Where moss grows over the stones of the well—
Everywhere
Sad voices are confiding secrets
Urging a woman, wakeful, troubled
To rise to find her loom . . .
Winding through the mountains beyond the screen
Alone in the cold night, where does the thread of her thoughts end?

Dark rain blows again against the west window
Why do they continue intermittently
To answer one another by the washing block?
I thought they would come in to welcome autumn
And in this temporary palace to lament by moonlight
A parting, painful beyond measure . . .

205
.

The Songs of Pin blithely tell
Of laughter, shouts in the lamplight by the bamboo fence
As children try to catch them—
Write that into the strings
And sound by sound the song becomes more bitter

CST 2175

·

CHIANG K'UEI

Nien nu chiao

Once I was posted to Wu-ling, the judicial capital of Hupei. By the ancient city wall, when spring floods and tall trees joined to touch heaven, two or three friends and I would, every day, drift in a boat, close to the lotus flowers, and drink. The scenery was profound, infinite, not like the human world. In autumn, when the lake was nearly dry, the lotus leaves grew eight to ten feet above the ground and we could sit in a row under them, completely shaded from the sun. A gentle breeze slowly moved green clouds. Where the leaves were sparse, we could surreptitiously glimpse revelers in fancy boats enjoying themselves. When I went back and forth to and from Wu-hsing, I would often linger among the lotus, and even drift on West Lake at night. The scenery was beyond compare, and so I wrote this.

One boat put red into confusion
When I came
With only ducks for company—
Thirty-six deserted pools
Draped in windblown finery—
Among green leaves, a breath of cool
Jade faces losing wine's flush
Moved by a sprinkle of rain among the reeds
To graceful dancing
Their cold fragrance flies into my verse

Their days ending
Green canopies stand tall
The flowers? Gone—
How could they leave so cruelly on the waves?
I fear the cold will claim even their dancing clothes

CHIANG K'UEI

And sorrow that the west wind sweeps the southern shore . . .
Under the drooping shade of lofty willows
Ancient fish blow up the waves
I have lingered among the flowers . . .
And under how many leaves
How many times along the road back?

CST 2177

Ling lung szu fan

In Yüeh, the old year drawing to an end,
hearing the flute and drum makes me despair.

Drums punctuate the cold night
Hanging lanterns—superficial signs of spring
Rush the season
I'm sick of all these places, there's not much to look forward to
In this sort of life—nor ever was
Chiang Yen already sang "Of Regrets"
And when I remember parting from you on the southern shore
Earth and heaven for ten thousand miles
Were I to live a hundred years
Would still be filled with misery

The willows of Yangchou hang on official roads
Where girls are changed for horses
Perfect features peek from doorways
But, waking from wine in bright moonlight
Dreams are ephemeral as the sound of the tide
Fine verse, just discourse—what use are they—
When the prize is a post at the edge of heaven!
Don't you see
Spring coming, all that matters is a lovely woman?

CST 2178 *

209

•

CHIANG K'UEI

Yang chou man

Winter Solstice, 1176, I pass through Wei-yang. Night frosts just be-
ginning, there's wild wheat everywhere. When I enter the city, all is
desolation. The water, cold, green for itself alone. Among the shadows
of evening echoes the doleful sound of taps. Melancholy thoughts wan-
der from present to past, and I compose this song. Old Ch'ien Yen
thinks it captures the sorrow of Shu-li.

South of the Huai, near the famous city
Chu-hsi was a fine place, once
To loose the saddle, spend a day or two
The spring wind passed . . . ten li
Of weeds green everything
Tartar horses coveted it, crossed the river, and
Left ruins by the pools and ancient trees—
Even now no one will talk of it
Slowly days fade
The horn, chill, clear, echoes
Within empty walls

Tu Lang valued its elegance
Were he to see it now, he'd be shocked
With all the skill of his cardamon song
Or the beauty of his green tower dreams
It would be hard to turn this into verse
Of the twenty-four bridges, some are left
And cold moonlight dancing on the waves—but not a sound
I marvel at red peonies beside the bridge
They blossom still, year after year—for whom?

CST 2180

Tu Lang, mentioned in Yang chou man, *is the T'ang dynasty poet Tu Mu:*

Parting

Lovely and lithe, just over thirteen
A cardamon sprout, the second month
In a spring breeze for ten li on the Yangchou road
Pearl shades are open—none can compare

Ch'an Chih Monastery Near Yangchou

The rain passes, a single cicada cries
Autumn sighs in pine and cassia
Green moss covers the stone steps
Where white birds once lingered
Evening clouds, ancient trees
The sun setting behind the small tower—
Who knows the way to Chu-hsi?
They sing and blow flutes in Yangchou

TU MU (802–853)

Expressing My Feelings

Dissolute, drinking by river and lakes
With girls so slim they could dance in my palm
Ten years passed like a dream in Yangchou
Making a name—in the row of green houses

A Message to Han Ch'o, the Yangchou Magistrate

Green mountains barely visible beyond the water
Autumn ending, but grass on the south bank not yet dry
Twenty-four bridges, a moonlit night—
Where is it lovely girls practice the flute?

TU MU (802–853)

CHIANG K'UEI

Tan huang liu

When I was posted to Ho-fei, south of the city there was a bridge with a red rail, west of it, an alley, very different from those south of the Yangtze. Only the shape and color of the willows that lined that road, the way they drooped, was familiar and lovely. I composed this song to relieve a stranger's despair.

The morning horn within the empty city walls
Echoes down the path where willows hang
On horseback in thin clothes, chilled, sick at heart
I try to look my fill at yellow down and tender green—
Old friends I knew South of the River

Isolated and alone just
When tomorrow morning it's Cold Hearth Festival again—
How much better when I brought wine
To Hsiao Ch'iao's house!
I fear when pear blossoms finish falling, it will be autumn
And should the swallows come
To ask for spring
There'll be only the pond still green

CST 2181

CHIANG K'UEI

An hsiang

In the winter of 1191 I went through the snow to visit Stone Lake. I stayed out the month and he asked me to write some new songs. These are the two I wrote. Stone Lake admired them so much he made a singer learn the words and music. The harmonies were lovely, so we named them An hsiang and Shu ying.

The moon, as usual
Count the times it shone for me
As I played the flute beside the plum
To wake her
We didn't care how cold, we'd climb and pluck
But Ho Hsün has grown old
Spring wind and song all but forgotten
I only feel it strange, sparse flowers beyond the bamboo fence
Should send cool fragrance here . . .

The River Country
Silent, lonely
I sigh to be so out of reach
Night snow piles up
A cup brings tears
Red flowers without words remind me of her
The place we held hands
A thousand trees above, West Lake, cold and green
Petals all blowing off—one by one
When again?

CST 2181

214

·

CHIANG K'UEI

Postscript

Once the music of tz'u was lost, the audience changed. As tz'u patterns became more strict, facility in handling them became more dazzling. Tz'u, written by people of similar education for each other, were increasingly absorbed with how things were being said, and said less and less, or were so obscure as to be almost inaccessible to an outsider.

Music had allowed variation. Meters came to be followed more and more slavishly. Out of touch with the songs of the courtesans, the language grew mannered. Gone was the sense of immediacy in the love poetry—the wine-flushed cheeks, the shadow of a swing sent over a wall by moonlight. Instead, there are the props of desire—dusty vanity cases, sidelong glances. By the time the dynasty fell tz'u had lost not only its music and its popular audience, but the spontaneity that had characterized it.

It became important again in the Ch'ing dynasty (1644–1911). Many anthologies of Sung tz'u were printed. Handbooks and manuals were compiled. With the help of these, and a Sung rhyme dictionary compiled in 1011, almost any educated person could write tz'u. To judge from the staggering number written, everyone did. All vestige of colloquial language and stylistic liberty was gone. The vernacular of the great Sung tz'u poets had in these five hundred years become the classical language of Sung tz'u, been codified, and become inseparable from the form itself. Like Liza Doolittle, tz'u had become respectable.

Under the Communists writing tz'u was deemed decadent once again, but for new reasons, and was forbidden by Mao Tse-tung. Mao himself, nevertheless, wrote quite a few.

Ch'in yüan ch'un

Snow

Written in 1936, the second month of the twenty-fourth year of the Republic

The northern landscape
A thousand miles of ice
Ten thousand miles of blowing snow
Inside the wall and out
Everything obscured by white
Up and down the great river
The waves lost at a stroke
The mountains: a dancing silver snake
The plateau: a white wax running elephant
Each rivaling heaven with its height—
But wait! One clear spring day
The red dress will emerge from the white wrapping
Especially seductive

Mountains and river lovely as this
Have enticed countless heroes to battle—and submit
Too bad the Ch'in emperor and Wu of Han
Couldn't write prose
Tai-tsung of T'ang, Kao-tsu of Sung
Weren't poets
The pride of heaven for a generation

Genghis Khan
Alone could bend a bow to shoot down a great eagle—
Yet, what is left?
Count the great gone in the ebb and flow of time
And then return to look at our day dawning

MAO TSE-TUNG

About the Poets

Li Yü (937–979)

The legend of Li Yü cannot be separated from his poems. More than biography, and probably less than historically accurate, it is an integral, but unspoken, dimension of his work, evoked by his images even when those are borrowed by later poets.

At twenty-five Li Yü, also known as Li Hou-chu (Li the last king) succeeded to the throne of the Southern T'ang, largest of the small kingdoms that characterized the period of disunity which followed the T'ang dynasty and preceeded the Sung. A poet, painter, calligrapher, and connoisseur himself, his queen a skilled musician, composer, and dancer, the court was an artist's paradise. The young king spent most of his energies on poetry, music, art, architecture, and love. Dire warnings of his ministers, though often well rewarded, went unheeded. "What use had we for the arts of war?"

As he was building his beautiful gardens, towers, and pagodas, writing his poems, the Sung was arming and consolidating its power. Eventually T'ai-tsu, the first Sung emperor, asked submission of his rivals, threatening invasion if he didn't get it. Li, who was expected to present himself personally in K'ai-feng, sent emissaries who recited his poems. This only angered T'ai-tsu who, among other things, considered his own verses superior. Li sent more envoys and tried to forget his troubles in the study of literature and Buddhism.

His love life was not turning out well either. An affair with his wife's sister, carried on too openly, contributed to the queen's untimely death. Li was shattered. Nevertheless, he married the sister. Contemporary gossip suggests the lady was a good deal less delightful as a wife than she had been as a mistress.

Out of patience with Li's excuses for not appearing at court, the Sung sent a punitive expedition, Nanking fell, and in 976 Li was carried off to the Sung capital at K'ai-feng. There he spent the remaining two years of his life under house arrest, in an alien landscape, remembering, regretting, writing—isolated, alone.

It is said that on seeing the tz'u that begins "Spring flowers, autumn moon" the second Sung emperor, T'ai-tsung, his power still a bit shaky, decided Li was a dangerous influence, and had him poisoned with a bottle of wine sent as a present on the occasion of Li's forty-second birthday.

Images of silence, loneliness, nostalgia for a lost past, carry the weight of his story—"a river of regrets, flowing east." It is his whole posture that lies at the heart of the tz'u tradition, and that is evoked time and time again in later poems by a line, a phrase, or an image.

LIN PU (967–1028)

A recluse, Lin lived in retirement near West Lake. Reputedly he threw his poems away as fast as he wrote them. When asked why, he explained that as he did not care for fame in his own time, why should he care about posterity? A few tz'u were copied by friends. Four survived.

FAN CHUNG-YEN (989–1052)

Fan was an extremely courageous and original thinker. He promoted scholarship in things besides the classics, and tried to reform the imperial examination to focus more on modern utilitarian subjects, less on poetry and literature. Fan's system of clan land trusts kept parcels of clan land together to provide schools, hospitals, old age homes, and other social and charitable services.

He was a protégé of Yen Shu, who, together with Ou-yang Hsiu, backed Fan's reforms. Under Emperor Jen-tsung, Fan held the highest cabinet position, the first from a simple background to do so. Orphaned young, he had been brought up by his mother and his mother's clan, reclaiming his father's clan only after he passed the imperial exam.

Fearless in his willingness to remonstrate with the emperor on a variety of issues, he was three times demoted. By the third time others began following his example. Finally recalled to a military post when the Hsi Hsia and Liao, tribal states to the north, threatened Sung, he fought three years at the front.

Brilliant though his ideas were, his reforms never got far. Those who had been his followers, after a brief flirtation with the big reform of Wang An-shih, became the conservatives of the next generation.

CHANG HSIEN (990–1078)

Chang passed the imperial examinations in Emperor Jen-tsung's time. He became head of a division of the judiciary department. In late years he traveled and led a leisured life. He left one collection of tz'u, noted for their vague beauty and, in particular, for the use of the word *shadow*. Much is made of his having continued to write love poetry well into his eighties and of the two singing girls he kept in his house for inspiration.

YEN SHU (991–1055)

In the political realm Yen was both prominent and successful. A child prodigy, he came to the attention of Emperor Jen-tsung, passed the examinations very young, and rose to the highest office. Among the people he supported were Ou-yang Hsiu and Fan Chung-yen. All three came to high positions from relatively simple families outside the bureaucracy. The Sung history describes both Yen Shu's prose and poetry as elegant. Some feel his tz'u are a bit too much so and border on the decadent.

Liu Yung (fl. 1034)

Liu came from a literary family in K'ai-feng. Talented both with words and music, he achieved fame as a song writer (tz'u) even before he took the imperial examinations. One of his early songs talks of trading fame for whispered song. According to legend, when Liu took the exam and was recommended to the emperor, the latter, remembering this song, asked, "Is this the songwriter Liu?" When he discovered it was, he said, "Let him write songs then," and failed him. Eventually, Liu did pass the exam but was turned down repeatedly for promotions.

Disappointment with his career is evident in many poems, though he often made light of it, styling himself a songwriter by imperial edict. In any event he spent most of his life in the singing houses with the girls who adored him. At this distance it is hard to know whether this was the cause or the result of his failed career. He died in poverty, and, the story goes, the girls raised the money for his funeral.

His language was colloquial and the words fitted wonderfully to the music—much of which he wrote himself. His songs were sung everywhere, among all classes of people, in village and city alike. About 206 tz'u survive, though it is thought there were many more.

ABOUT THE POETS

CHANG SHEN (992–1077)

Chang was a high minister in the reign of Jen-tsung. He left no collection.

OU-YANG HSIU (1007–1072)

From a simple background, and largely self-educated, Ou-yang rose to the highest government posts. His political success was short-lived and his political influence limited, but his intellectual and literary contributions were immense and lasting. As a historian, he was adamant about preserving evidence, past and present, and shielding it from politically expedient distortion; he collected and organized ancient stone and bronze inscriptions; he pressed successfully for preserving contemporary source material. Among a vast range of varied accomplishments are the writing of the official T'ang dynasty history and an important role in compiling an annotated bibliography of the 3,445 titles in the imperial library. In the realm of ideas he originated the notion of diverse interpretations of the classics, opening the door to the great age of neo-Confucian philosophy.

One of the eight prose masters of T'ang and Sung, Ou-yang was active in the reform of the prose style. His own prose was considered a model down to modern times. His informal essays on poets and poetry, "poetry chats," became the prototype for an important genre of literary criticism. A prolific and highly esteemed poet, his collection includes 156 tz'u. These were twice used against him by political opponents, who, despite the fact that he was exonerated of the charges both times, successfully shattered his political career with accusations of incest.

Residue from this scandal, as well as the outspoken sensuality of the poems themselves, induced the more moralistic Southern Sung defenders of Ou-yang's reputation—to whom his tz'u were an embarrassment—to dismiss some of them, long after his death, as not his. The result, persistent confusion in questions of attribution, is particularly ironic as it is based on distortion of historical evidence of precisely the sort Ou-yang had sought to discourage.

Su Shih (1037–1101)

Su was a man of prodigious talents, whose life was dogged by incredible bad luck. Considered the foremost poet of the period, he was an outstanding painter, prose stylist, and calligrapher as well. After he passed the chin shih imperial exam for entry into government, he did brilliantly on a higher exam, at which only a handful succeeded. The second exam should have advanced his career by ten years. It never happened.

Twenty-seven months of official mourning for each parent required his return to Szechuan for two extended periods. By the time he came back to the capital to take up that career his faction was being pushed out to provincial posts. Except for a brief hiatus twenty years later, the opposing faction, Wang An-shih's New Laws party, continued to hold sway for the rest of Su's life. Consequently, he was mostly in exile, often in remote and disease-ridden places, in conditions of terrible poverty.

He made do. Far from becoming embittered by his experiences, he developed the very positive Zen philosophy so evident in his poems, taking joy in a host of small things—a sudden shower, some spring herbs, a glass of wine.

Although political success eluded them all, the three Sus, as they are known, all left their mark. Su Shih's father, Su Hsün, was a self-styled scholar who never passed the examination, influential nonetheless, particularly in the reform of prose style. Su Hsün, Su Shih

224

himself, and his younger brother, Su Ch'e (Tzu-yu), are all among the eight prose masters of T'ang and Sung. The mother, an educated woman and devout Buddhist, ran a clothing store to support the family.

The attachment of the Su brothers, Su Shih and Su Ch'e, to one another is legendary and lasted a lifetime. Inseparable in their youth, after they passed the exams (Ou-yang Hsiu was examiner), they were almost never together again, thanks to the vicissitudes of their ill-fated careers. Many poems were exchanged, the most touching, perhaps, those written on Moon Festival when they felt their separation most keenly.

Su Shih's first provincial post was Hangchou where the flooding of West Lake was a perennial problem. In the three years he was there a disastrous flood was followed by famine the next year and locusts the year after. His work on relief won him the lasting affection of the people. Late in his life he was to return to West Lake, dredge the roots and silt from the lake to help control flooding, and with these build a dyke, with sluices for irrigation. He planted trees to hold the dyke, made a walkway with pavilions of the top. The dyke has controlled flooding for a thousand years; the causeway, where one can still stroll today, is an outstanding scenic attraction in a region that boasts many.

Life as a provincial official might have suited him, but time and again Wang's successors tried to make an example of him, picking through his old writings, accusing him of slander. As he often satirized authority, it was not hard to make the accusations stick. Once, he was within hours of being executed. The few times he was recalled to the capital, honored, promoted, it was only to be hounded out again on the same old charges. When a provincial post seemed still too close for comfort, he was banished to some remote spot, ultimately, the malarial island of Hainan. Recalled after four years, he died of dysentery on his way home.

In their zeal, his enemies continued to try to discredit him, even after he was dead. His books were banned, his calligraphy destroyed. But before long the emperor himself was reciting his poems, collecting his paintings and calligraphy. 2,400 poems and some 300 tz'u survive.

Chou Pang-yen (1056–1121)

Su Shih detached tz'u from music; Chou Pang-yen, considered the greatest musician and song writer of his day, briefly made tz'u songs again. About 60 of the 114 patterns he used were to his own musical compositions.

Chou grew up in Hangchou, one of the most beautiful regions of China, which may account for his vivid appreciation of nature. He bypassed the imperial examination while a student in the capital by presenting a rhyme-prose composition on K'ai-feng, celebrating the capital city and the accomplishments of the dynasty. It won him a post in the academy where he had, until then, been a student. From then on he held mostly academic positions, both in the provinces and the capital, the highest being Director of the Imperial Music Bureau.

Shortly after he died, the Jurched seized the north, kidnapped the emperor, and threw China into turmoil. Consequently, many of Chou's poems were lost. For the same reason, or perhaps because he was a very private person, very little biographical material survives. The two collections of his work that date from the Sung dynasty, compiled by others after his death, overlap; texts of individual poems differ.

His abstruse and elegant style was particularly admired in the

226

·

Southern Sung and again in the Ch'ing dynasty (1644–1911), when his tz'u once more became very influential. Even after the music was lost, his patterns continued to be used.

Chao Chi (Emperor Hui-tsung; 1082–1135)

An ill-advised alliance with the Jurched to defeat the Khitans ended Hui-tsung's reign (1101–1126) and, with it, the Northern Sung dynasty. As soon as the Khitans were out of the way, the Jurched double-crossed the Sung, marched on the capital, K'ai-feng, sacked the city, and eventually carried off Hui-tsung, his heir, Ch'in-tsung, and a large part of the Sung court.

The Jurched started their own dynasty in the north, while a son of Hui-tsung who had escaped capture tried to rally what was left of the Sung court and establish himself in the south. When the dust settled, there was the Chin dynasty with its own emperor plus two Sung emperors as prisoners in the north, and Kao-tsung, the first emperor of Southern Sung, in Hangchou. Kao-tsung made no great efforts to regain the north or free his father and brother—for obvious reasons. The partition was to last, a focus of both politics and poetry, until the Mongol conquest.

In his quarter century as emperor Hui-tsung was weak, profligate in his use of public funds, prone to manipulation by a scheming prime minister who pandered to his dissolute tastes, but, at the same time, a very great patron of the arts. A man of both talent and taste, he was respected as a poet, painter, and calligrapher, as well as a collector. Not only his poetry but some of his painting and calligraphy survive. He died, still a prisoner of the Chin, nine years after his capture. The tz'u this last of the Northern Sung emperors wrote, at the end of his life, are, ironically, reminiscent of those Li Yü wrote, under similar circumstances, when a prisoner of the first.

Li Ch'ing-chao (1084–c. 1155)

Generally acknowledged to be China's foremost woman poet, Li had all the virtues of the perfect Sung gentleman: she was accomplished in music, painting, and calligraphy, a collector of rare books and antiquities, author of various prose works, including some of the earliest works of tz'u criticism, and, already in her lifetime, highly respected as a poet. Neo-Confucian ideas of the time considered even literacy subversive to feminine virtue. Many women of her class were illiterate, hobbled about on bound feet, and lived lives of boredom and intrigue within the inner chambers, longing for absent—or errant—husbands.

Educated at home in K'ai-feng in a family of scholars, Li came in contact with the intellectuals of her father's circle—which included Su Shih—and later her husband's. To what degree she moved freely in this male world, or how much she was accepted in it, is hard to establish. It was all, certainly, unusual. How it was even possible is a mystery.

At seventeen she was married to Chao Ming-ch'eng, a scholar-official from a family even more prominent than her own but of the opposing, Wang An-shih, faction. From all accounts, including her own, the marriage was idyllic, though again unusual. Li shared Chao's passion for collecting rare books and antiquities. They collaborated on a book of stone and bronze inscriptions (*Chin shih lu*), attributed to her husband, to which she wrote an autobiographical postscript after his death (both extant). Every penny they could scrape together was spent acquiring some rare object, manuscript, painting, or calligraphy. The collection grew to be the best and most complete of the time. They had no children.

She was in her mid-forties when K'ai-feng fell to the Chin. Trying to salvage what they could, Li and her husband fled south, just ahead of the advancing Chin, to one place after another, always just

228
·

too late. The bulk of the collection was burned in their house in Ch'ing-chou in 1127. They still carried twenty-thousand books with them, but eventually these too were lost. It is a typical wartime story.

In the midst of this turmoil Chao Ming-ch'eng died. About the same time, Li's father was disgraced. Within a period of two years her whole life had collapsed.

She tried to join various relations, first in Hung-chou and then in T'ai-chou. Both places fell to the Chin before she reached them. Somehow she continued south, in the wake of the Sung court, and eventually reached Hangchou.

There is evidence that she remarried. For nine centuries scholars have argued the point. Her defenders say it was impossible; a woman of good family could not have done such a thing. Besides, her love poems, always assumed to have been written to Chao Ming-ch'eng, and the poems of grief after his death, are so moving, it was both culturally and aesthetically unacceptable for her not to remain faithful to his memory. To rehabilitate her honor, in Confucian terms— remarriage of widows was frowned on—they claimed the records had been fabricated by male poets, jealous of her reputation.

If she did remarry (1132), it was to a lout whom she later accused of embezzlement. Judged guilty, he was sent away; it was she who was sent to prison. Denouncing a husband was the more serious crime. The intercession of a relative won her release after nine days.

Whatever the story, with no father, brother, or son to protect her and provide for her, her life was probably miserable. She is thought to have been homeless and in poverty at the end. Very little is known; even the year of her death is uncertain. The official history of the Sung dynasty, written in the succeeding Yüan, has no biography for her; she is mentioned in her father's.

Of the twelve volumes (chüan) of poetry and prose attributed to her in the Sung Bibliography (preface dated 1151), six were collections of tz'u. What survives is seventy-eight tz'u, half of which are of dubious authorship, and a handful of other writings. Even with so little extant, she is ranked with Su Shih and Hsin Ch'i-chi among the greatest tz'u poets of the Sung.

LU YU (1125–1210)

Descended from a line of scholar-officials that had gone into retirement between the T'ang dynasty and the Sung, Lu was the fifth generation of his family to pass the examination and enter the Sung bureaucracy. But that path was far from being made easy for him.

He was born two years before the Jurched invasion. His father was violently opposed to peace with the Chin. Lu grew up equally hawkish and was repeatedly failed in the examinations and later frustrated in getting appointments because the peace party was in power, and the prime minister particularly disliked Lu's father.

The war party had a brief chance when Hsiao-tsung became emperor in 1162, but a crushing military defeat for Southern Sung again put Lu's ideas out of favor—more or less permanently. He continued throughout his long life to voice sympathy with his countrymen under Chin rule, express shame at appeasement, sound a call to arms, in both poems and memorials, almost obsessively; the position continued to be unpopular.

His career, though long, was therefore not a great success. Four times he was thrown out of office on charges of drunkenness and irresponsibility. As a result, he styled himself the "uninhibited patriarch." He enjoyed a brief retirement early on in a house he built on Mirror Lake, was recalled to office, spent nine years in provincial posts in Szechuan, followed by more of the same elsewhere. In 1190 he retired to Shao-hsing and lived on a meager pension for the rest of his life, returning to Hangchou only twice.

His personal life was difficult. At twenty he was married to a cousin, T'ang Wan, with whom he was, briefly, extremely happy. His mother became "dissatisfied" with the daughter-in-law, and forced Lu to send her home and divorce. A second marriage was immediately arranged to a lady who presumably better pleased the mother and with whom he had six sons. Regret for his separation from his first wife became a recurrent theme in his poems and tz'u. *Ch'ai t'ou feng* records a chance meeting many years after the divorce. The last poem he wrote about her was written when Lu was eighty-four and T'ang Wan had been dead half a century.

Lu is considered the greatest shih poet of Southern Sung, in the tradition of T'ang poets Tu Fu and Po Chü-i. He is also the most prolific, even though he destroyed everything he'd written before he was forty-one, presumably because the early poems were in the ornate, elegant, Chiang-hsi style which he abandoned. He left 9,000 shih and 130 tz'u. His prose compositions include an important travel diary. Alongside the patriotic poems are many simple, personal observations of everyday life, immensely diverse, finely observed, and masterfully rendered.

HSIN CH'I-CHI (1140–1207)

Hsin was born in north China when the Chin had already controlled that part of the country for thirteen years. For ethnic Chinese in the north, it was a period of privation, humiliation, and foreign rule. For the Chinese of the south, and for the court which had fled there after the collapse of Northern Sung, it was a period of prosperity, flourishing trade, science, arts, letters, and, at the same time, appeasement, tribute, and political humiliation.

As a young man Hsin moved south. After distinguishing himself in some minor skirmishes against the Chin, he joined the Southern Sung court. His career was the traditional one of public service, but his opposition to the policy of appeasement and his hawkish schemes to recapture the north gained little support. The most prolific tz'u poet of the age—over 600 are extant—many of his poems reflect disappointment and frustration over the partition of China.

After twenty stormy years in official posts, he retired "to dream about the time of my youth spent in the saddle, and be immersed in the poetry and classics of the ancients" (Lo, *Hsin Ch'i-chi*, p. 32). It was in this last period of his life, spent as a recluse, that he wrote most of his poetry.

His tz'u are infinitely varied in both subject and style, ranging from highly allusive and complex to simple and humorous. He is considered to have carried further the grand tradition of Su Shih and is thought by many to be the greatest tz'u poet of Southern Sung.

CHIANG K'UEI (1155?–1221?)

Chiang composed the music for the seventeen new tz'u patterns he initiated. The score is extant. It is a very rare example of early Chinese musical notation, and virtually impossible to interpret.

Born into the family of a scholar-official, Chiang tried several times to pass the imperial examinations and to enter the bureaucracy by other means. All failed. A commoner all his life, he was none the less, according to an autobiographical essay, known to many of the great poet-statesmen of his day—Yang Wan-li, Chu Hsi, Hsin Ch'i-chi, Fan Ch'eng-ta, among others—as an accomplished musician, poet, and art critic. To live he depended on patronage and the occasional sale of his calligraphy. Always poor, his poverty was extreme at the end, as he had outlived his patrons.

Major Poetic Genres by Dynasty

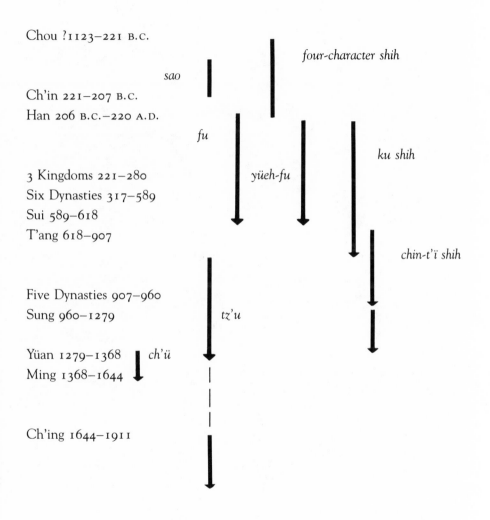

Chou ?1123–221 B.C.

four-character shih

sao

Ch'in 221–207 B.C.
Han 206 B.C.–220 A.D.

fu

ku shih

3 Kingdoms 221–280
Six Dynasties 317–589
Sui 589–618
T'ang 618–907

yüeh-fu

chin-t'ï shih

Five Dynasties 907–960
Sung 960–1279

tz'u

Yüan 1279–1368   *ch'ü*
Ming 1368–1644

Ch'ing 1644–1911

Glossary

An hsiang—dark fragrance, paired with shu ying—sparse shadows, is from a couplet in a poem about the form and smell of plum blossoms by Lin Pu.

Autumn wheel, the moon.

Autumn wind, see Chang Han.

Ch'an Chih Monastery, Ch'an (Zen) wisdom monastery.

Chang Ch'ang (d. 48 B.C.), Han dynasty scholar whose fetish was to put kohl on his wife's eyebrows.

Chang Chi-ying, Chang Han (q.v.).

Chang Han (Chang Chi-ying, c. 258–319), while serving as an official in Loyang was reminded by the autumn wind of seasonal delicacies of his home in Kiangsu, lu fish and a type of edible seaweed. He immediately resigned and went home, on the grounds that seeking fame and titles was futile—one should enjoy life. Actually, he used this as a pretext to leave office before imperial favor shifted.

Chang Kung-fu, a poet and aristocrat who lived and entertained lavishly.

Chang-tai Road, the red light district of Ch'ang-an, therefore also used as a generic term for any red light district.

Chang T'a-k'e, identity not known, perhaps a relative of Chang Kung-fu.

Ch'ang-an, the capital in the Former Han dynasty (206 B.C.–A.D. 9) and the T'ang (618–907), often used in poetry for the current capital.

Chao and Li, families related to the Imperial Han who represent the height of luxurious living.

Chao-hsiang, where T'ang dynasty Emperor Hsüan-tsung (r. 713–755) and his mistress, Yang Kuei-fei, appreciated flowers together.

Chao-yang, the palace built for Flying Swallow (q.v.) by Emperor Ch'eng.

che-ku, see t'i-chüeh.

cheng, a string instrument of ancient origin that is plucked, something like a zither.

ch'i ch'i, onomatopoetic sound made by crickets, meaning "cold, cold."

Chia-hsüan, Hsin Ch'i-chi styled himself Chia-hsüan (meaning "farmer's studio") from the name of his estate.

Chiang Yen (444–505) had dreamed as a young man that he was given a multicolored brush. He attributed his poetic skill to that dreamed image. When late in life he dreamed the brush was taken back, he could never write again. He is the author of several famous rhyme-prose compositions.

Ch'iao, surname of two sisters, famous for their beauty in the time of the Three Kingdoms. One was married to the king of Wu (Sun Ch'üan), the other to his illustrious general, Chou Yü.

Ch'ien-t'ang, Hangchou.

Ch'ien Yen, the poet Hsiao Te-tsao, a friend of Chiang K'uei.

Chin, Jurched conquerors of north China, responsible for the partition of the Sung Empire into the Chin (1115–1234) in the north, and Southern Sung (1127–1279) in the south.

Chin-ling, Nanking.

ch'in, a stringed musical instrument roughly four feet long, similar to the zither. In ancient times it had five strings, now it has seven. Playing it is thought to cultivate character, help to understand morality, supplicate gods, enhance life, and enrich learning. Already Confucius' favorite, the ch'in is the scholar's instrument.

The Ch'ing, a river.

Ch'ing-ming, a festival devoted to sweeping the graves of the ancestors and going into the country to enjoy nature: a picnic, a boat ride, "treading the green." There was a general exodus from cities such as Hangchou on Ch'ing-ming, and people stayed out all day, women as well as men. It is the only popular festival tied to the solar calendar, the 105th day after Winter Solstice. Reference to Ch'ing-ming, as to Cold Food Festival that immediately precedes it, is often simply a reference to the season: the end of spring.

Chiu-chiang, place to which T'ang dynasty poet, Po Chü-i (772–846) was banished. There he wrote one of his most prized poems, *P'i-p'a Song*, which describes the meeting of the exiled poet and an aging singer, both far from the capital and past glory. On a moonlit night, the strangers exchange stories, share the music and their common misfortune, as each drifts in a boat at Chiu-chiang.

Chou Yü, general and strategist of the state of Wu in the Three Kingdoms era (220–280), a glamorous figure, responsible for the defeat of Ts'ao Ts'ao at the battle of Red Cliff.

Chu-hsi, a pavilion with beautiful surroundings in a temple east of Yangchou. The whole area was once known as the pleasure capital.

Ch'u, designates a region in south China, from the name of the ancient state of Ch'u in that region. The courtesans of the state of Ch'u reputedly starved themselves because the king's taste was for slim waists.

Ch'u gorge, a place near Kao-t'ang terrace. Mention of Ch'u gorge usually alludes to the story told in the *Kao-t'ang fu* (q.v.). It is often a euphemism for a sexual encounter.

Chung-chou, Honan province, where the Northern Sung capital Pien-ching (K'ai-feng) was. In Li Ch'ing-chao's poem it is a reference to the former capital, K'ai-feng.

chüeh-chü, see shih.

Cold Food Festival, commemorates the burning of a wise man by a foolish monarch. All fires were extinguished for three days. Ceremonial "new fire" was then passed from torch to torch. Cold Food Festival immediately precedes Ch'ing-ming (q.v.), and mention of either festival is often simply a reference to the season: late spring.

Cold Hearth Festival, Cold Food Festival (q.v.).

Day of No Fire, Cold Food Festival (q.v.).

Double Ninth, a festival, the ninth day of the ninth lunar month, a day for an excursion to high ground to write poetry, drink wine, view chrysanthemums.

Fan, or round fan, alludes to a poem by Lady Pan, imperial concubine to Emperor Ch'eng of Han (r. 32–8 B.C.). In the poem she compares herself to a round silk fan, much prized in the summer, put away when the weather turns cool.

Feng-ch'ih, literally, Phoenix Pond, but perhaps a designation for the cabinet.

Feng T'ang, upright official of the Han dynasty in the reign of Emperor Wen (202–157 B.C.). He dared to publicly criticize the emperor for dismissing a good minister. Feng T'ang prevailed, and the minister, magistrate of Yün-chung, was reinstated.

First Full Moon, Lantern Festival (q.v.).

Flying mirror, the moon.

Flying Swallow, Chao Fei-yen (d. 6 B.C.), favorite of Emperor Ch'eng of the Han dynasty. She was famed as a dancer; so light, the story goes, she could dance on a man's palm.

Fo Li (r. 424–451), pet name of the third emperor of Northern Wei, feared for his cruelty and boldness.

fu, poetic form sometimes called rhyme-prose that became important in the second century B.C.

fu-sang, a tree that grows in the east, where the sun rises.

Garu wood, fragrant wood of the lign-aloes.

General of a thousand victories, Li Ling (d. 74 B.C.), a brilliant Han dynasty general, who, after many victories, was overpowered by a superior force and captured. Chinese generals were not supposed to be captured or defeated. The story was made famous by Han historian Ssu-ma Ch'ien, who, as a result of speaking out in Li's defense, had the choice of death or castration as punishment. Li is often mentioned with Su Wu, an envoy who was detained by the Hsiung-nu for nineteen years, and then was able to return to China, while Li was not.

Golden beast, an incense burner. These were usually decorative objects made of precious material, often in animal shapes.

Golden Valley, a park outside Loyang that belonged to the poet-official Shih Ch'ung (249–300), famous for his ostentatious banquets.

Green houses, brothels.

Han-chung, place where Liu Pang, founder of Han, established his empire.

Heng-yang, a town where, the Chinese believe, the migrating geese always stop on their way further south.

Ho, a famous musician in the reign of T'ang dynasty emperor Hsüan-tsung (r. 713–756).

Ho Fang-hui (1063–1120), the poet Ho Chu.

Ho-fei, city in Anhwei.

Ho Hsün (d. c. 527), a poet who wrote about plum blossoms.

Hsiang-ju, the poet Ssu-ma Hsiang-ju (q.v.).

Hsiao and Hsiang, rivers, the Hsiao is a tributary of the Hsiang, and perhaps for this reason their juncture is thought to be a place where thoughts meet.

Hsiao Ch'iao, younger of two sisters known for their beauty in the Three Kingdoms era. She was married to Chou Yü (q.v.). The proper name of a historic beauty is often used to designate a beautiful woman.

Hsiao Man, name of the concubine of the T'ang dynasty poet Po Chü-i (772–846), probably used by Su Shih to refer to his own mistress. Po Chü-i, like Su Shih, had at one time been prefect of Hangchou.

Hsün Ching (Hsün Fen-ch'ien), according to legend kept his feverish dying wife cool with his own body. When she died, he grieved that the same sort of beauty would not come again, and pined away.

Hu, a name for foreigners, usually referring to Mongol or Tartar tribes.

The Huai, a river that begins in Honan, runs through Anhwei, to the Kiangsu coast.

Huai-nan, a region south of the Huai.

Jade Ring, Yang Kuei-fei, favorite of Emperor Hsüan-tsung of T'ang (r. 713–756).

Kao-t'ang, refers to the Kao-t'ang fu, an early Han rhyme-prose composition. In it the courtier Sung Yü tells King Hsiang of Ch'u (r. 298–265 B.C.) about the encounter of a former king with the goddess of Wu Mountain. Mention of any aspect of this story is usually a euphemism for a sexual encounter.

Kao-yang, a reference to the Kao-t'ang fu.

Lantern Festival, last and most spectacular of the festivals associated with New Year (q.v.). Celebrated at the first full moon, the fourteenth, fifteenth, and sixteenth day of the first moon, it was a sort of carnival. Every house was decorated with lanterns; the richer the house, the finer and more numerous the lanterns. Those decorating the palace, of course, were the most astonishing. The lanterns were in different colors and shapes and came from all over China. Many were activated to move or spin by ingenious methods using heat or water. Particularly prized were lanterns from Suchou, made of glass in five colors, and those from

Fu-chou, in white jade. In K'ai-feng large dragons were made of wicker, covered with cloth, lit from the inside by many lanterns, and carried by dancers. On the streets of Hangchou, in Southern Sung, there was every sort of entertainment—theater, opera, dance, puppets. Markets, shops, food stands, and restaurants stayed open all night. The festival marked one of the few occasions women could leave the inner quarters. Streets were crowded with people of all kinds, upper-class women were in carriages, upper-class men on horseback, hoi polloi on foot.

Lao Tzu, the philosopher to whom is attributed the *Tao-te ching.* Whether he was a real historical figure is not clear. The teachings of Lao Tzu are often interpreted as the philosophy of the recluse who has withdrawn from contamination of worldly affairs to become one with nature. But the name *Lao Tzu* literally means "old man" and might be used by a poet to refer to himself.

Laurel, the Chinese see a rabbit, a toad, and a laurel tree in the moon.

li, a unit of length, 360 paces or about 1/3 mile.

Liang-chou, one of the nine provinces of Ancient China.

Liu Lang, Liu Pei, distant relation of the Han imperial family, founder of Shu in the Three Kingdoms period (220–280).

Long Gate, usually refers to the story of Empress Ch'en. When Emperor Wu of Han (r. 140–86 B.C.) found a new favorite, he sent the empress to Long Gate Palace. From there, she commissioned the poet Ssu-ma Hsiang-ju to write a rhyme-prose composition that would reinstate her to favor. The story has two different endings: one, that he did and it did, the other, that he did and it did not.

Lu Chi (261–303), Chin dynasty poet, author of an essay on literature that is pivotal in Chinese literary criticism.

Lu fish, see Chang Han.

lü-shih, see shih.

Mid-Autumn Festival, Moon Festival (q.v.).

Mien, old name for Han-yang.

Mo-ch'ou, name of a girl in an old folk song; roughly translated, the name means "carefree."

Mo-ling, ancient name for what is now Nanking.

Moon, a goddess lives there with attendant beings. In it the Chinese see a rabbit, a toad, and a laurel tree. It unites the gaze of parted lovers.

Moon Festival, fifteenth day of the eighth moon. The practice was to view the moon with family, friend, or lover, drink and listen to music.

Mt. T'ien, both a mountain and a mountain range in northwest China. In Lu Yu's *Su chung ching,* probably a metaphor for his dreams of reconquering the north. The literal meaning of *t'ien* is heaven.

Nan Shan, South Mountain.

Nan Shan tiger, alludes to a story about the Han general Li Kuang who, whenever he heard there was a tiger in the area, went out to shoot it personally.

New Year, the Chinese lunar New Year, marked by a string of holidays. Toward the end of the old year offerings are made to various household gods, doorways are swept and watered, images of door gods of the old year come down, new ones go up along with red streamers to welcome spring. New Year's eve everyone stays home, shops and markets close. Then come three days of family visits. The real festivities are at the first full moon, Lantern Festival (q.v.).

Nien-nu, famous singing girl of the T'ang dynasty (618–907).

P'an-p'an, a singer and dancer, concubine of Chang Chien-feng (735–800). He built Swallow Tower (q.v.) for her. After he died she lived there alone, faithful to his memory.

Pei-mang, graveyard near Loyang and, by extension, any graveyard.

P'eng-ch'eng, Hsü-chou.

p'i-p'a, a plucked lute with four strings, often mentioned to allude to Wang Chao-chün (q.v.). The instrument has been known since the third century B.C.

Po-ku, Su Ch'ien, a distant cousin of Su Shih who stayed with Su for three years.

Post station, a rest house for travelers, especially official couriers.

Red Cliff, scene of a famous battle of the Three Kingdoms era (220–280), where Chou Yü burned Ts'ao Ts'ao's fleet (see Sun Ch'üan).

Red tower, singing house, brothel.

River of Stars, the Milky Way.

Roc (*p'eng*), a fabulous bird associated with immortality. The story is from Chuang Tzu.

Row of green houses, singing houses, brothels.

sheng, a wind instrument of southeast Asian origin that can produce many notes at once. It consists of a number of pipes with keyholes that are fingered.

shih, earliest verse form in Chinese, used in the folk songs and ballads of the *Shih ching* (The book of songs), supposedly compiled by Confucius. It has a four character end-stopped line. Later developments were *ku-shih* (ancient style shih), used from the second century on, which has lines of equal length, usually five or seven words; total length of the poem is not prescribed. In the T'ang dynasty *ch'in-t'i shih* (new style shih) flourished. New style prescribed almost everything:

lü-shih, regulated verse, has eight lines, verbal parallelism in the middle two couplets, fixed tonal pattern, single rhyme, uniform line length, either five or seven characters, throughout the poem.
chüeh-chü, four line, constant line length of five or seven characters, a single rhyme and prescribed tone pattern.
p'ai-lu, similar to lü-shih, but can be any length and may use more than one rhyme.

The Shuang, a river.

Shu-li, a song in the Confucian classic, *Shih ching* (The book of songs), which describes the desolation of a former capital.

Shu ying, sparse shadows, from a line in a poem by Lin Pu (see an hsiang).

Silver River, Milky Way.

Singing girl, a courtesan, a prostitute, whose talents included singing.

Singing house, a brothel. The higher the social level of the clientele, the more trained and talented as musicians and singers were the singing girls. The most talented and refined were high class, celebrated, courtesans, who lived in luxury and were invited in the highest circles of the court.

Six Dynasties (317–589), period of disunion. It was marked by rival houses vying for power, a division between north and south, a decline in Confucian values, the rise of Buddhism. Many intellectuals in this period withdrew from public life, and much great eremitic poetry was written.

Sky Wolf, a constellation.

Songs of Pin, one section of the Confucian classic, the *Shih ching* (The book of songs).

Ssu-ma Hsiang-ju (c. 179–117 B.C.), poet to whom is attributed the rhyme-prose composition on Long Gate Palace commissioned by Empress Ch'en (q.v.).

Stone Lake, the poet Fan Ch'eng-ta (1126–1193).

Su Ch'in, a Warring States (403–221 B.C.) figure who tried to unite six kingdoms to resist Ch'in (221–207 B.C.).

Sun Ch'üan (182–252), founder of Wu in the Three Kingdoms period. His general, Chou Yü, defeated Ts'ao Ts'ao in the battle of Red Cliff. Among his many exploits, was capturing a tiger during a hunt.

Sung-chiang, see Yellow Ears.

Sung Yü, courtier to King Hsiang of Ch'u (r. 298–265 B.C.), thought to be a follower of Ch'ü Yüan (322–295 B.C.), a poet official who drowned himself when his sovereign didn't make use of him.

Sunny Spring, traditionally considered the most refined of songs, appreciated only by the most sophisticated. It was extremely difficult to sing.

Swallow Tower, built for P'an-p'an (q.v.).

T'ao Ch'ien, poet (365–427), one of the great nature poets of the Six Dynasties era, who was happy to eke out a meager living from the land rather than serve in office.

Three Kingdoms (220–280), period when Wu, Wei, and Shu vied for supremacy.

t'i-chüeh, a bird, sometimes translated as shrike. Che-ku, t'i-kuei, and tu-chüan are similar birds. These are variously translated partridge, goatsucker, nightjar, and cuckoo. They sing at equinox and their cry is onomatopoetic to "you can't go home." The tu-chüan is also thought of in relation to a story about Tu Yu, a legendary king of Shu, who, when his minister Pieh Ling was away, had an affair with Pieh's wife. When the story came out, the king died of shame. It is said he turned into a cuckoo (che-ku, now sometimes called tu-yu) that weeps at the end of spring and sheds tears of blood.

t'i-kuei, see t'i-chüeh.

T'ien Sui, T'ang dynasty recluse poet Lu Kuei-meng.

Ts'ao, Ts'ao Ts'ao, founder of the Wei dynasty, rival of Liu Pei and Sun Ch'üan in the Three Kingdoms (Wei, Shu, and Wu) era (220–280).

tu-chüan, see t'i-chüeh.

Tu Lang, "young Tu," the poet Tu Mu (q.v.).

Tu Mu, T'ang dynasty poet (802–853).

Tung-ling, in the Ch'in dynasty (221–207 B.C.) Shao Ping held the title of

Marquis of Tung-ling. In the succeeding Han dynasty he lost his wealth and raised melons.

tz'u, poetic form that probably emerged about 700, originally words to songs written to new or old music. New lyrics continued to be written to the same tunes. Eventually the music was lost and the words were written to metric patterns established from earlier tz'u. The patterns retained the names of the original songs. Full flowering of tz'u came in the Sung dynasty.

Tz'u-yu, Su Ch'e, Su Shih's younger brother.

Wang and Hsieh, names of two noble families descended from two prime ministers of the Eastern Chin dynasty (317–420). By the T'ang dynasty (618–907) the families had lost their position.

Wang Chao-chün (also known as Wang Chiang and Ming-fei), courtesan under Han Yüan-ti (r. 48–32 B.C.). According to legend, the emperor selected his concubines from portraits. She refused to bribe the painter to render her more beautiful than she was, as the others did, and so never came to his notice. Eventually, she was given to a Hsiung-nu chieftain to cement a treaty. When she came to take leave of the emperor, he realized what he had missed. The earliest poem to mention her singing to the p'i-p'a is third century. Hers is also the green grave in the desert.

Wang-ch'uan, the name of the estate of T'ang dynasty poet Wang Wei (701–761), a prominent minister of state.

Wei-yang, variant name for Yangchou.

Wu, name of an ancient state in the region of modern Chekiang and Kiangsu. Also the name of one of the Three Kingdoms.

Wu-chung, Suchou.

Wu-ling, a city in Hupei. In the story *Peach Blossom Spring* by the poet T'ao Ch'ien (q.v.), a fisherman happens on a secluded village where the inhabitants have lived for generations out of time, undisturbed by political upheavals—a sort of Shangri-la. Once he leaves the village, neither he

246

nor anyone else can ever find it again. As the fisherman's home is Wu-ling, mention of the city suggests his story.

Wu-men, old name for Suchou.

Wu sword, swords made in the Wu region are supposedly the best. Tapping the sword alludes to the story of a Warring States figure, Feng Hsüan, who resorted to such a device to attract the attention of his leader.

wu-t'ung, a tree, last to lose its leaves in autumn, a symbol of the passage of time, the end of profusion, and, by extension, of youth.

Yang-kuan, mountain pass in Kansu and the title of a famous farewell song based on a quatrain by T'ang poet Wang Wei (701–761).

> In Wei-ch'eng, early rain settles the dust
>
> The willow by the inn sprouts new green
>
> Come, let's drink another cup of wine
>
> West of Yang-kuan, there'll be no friends.

Yellow Ears, name of a dog that belonged to Chin dynasty poet Lu Chi (261–303). When Lu Chi was posted to Loyang, he sent Yellow Ears home to Sung-chiang with a message tied round his neck.

Yellow Tower, built by Su Shih over a city gate at Hsu-chou where he served in 1078.

Yen tzu, mountain where the sun sets.

Yi, the Yi River, alludes to the story of Ching K'o, hired by the Prince of Yen to assassinate the first emperor of Ch'in (r. 227–207 B.C.). Ching K'o was given a banquet on the banks of the Yi. To a five-stringed lute he sang:

> The wind sighs, sighs
> Yi waters run cold
> The hero once gone
> Will not return

Yü-hang gate, at Hangchou.

Yü Hsin (512–580), poet and official of the Liang dynasty (502–556). He lived through many upheavals and spent a large part of his life exiled to north China, where he wrote a famous lament for the southern region of his birth.

yüan-yang, mandarin ducks, male and female, symbols of conjugal bliss, often embroidered on bridal quilts.

Yüeh, name of an ancient state in modern Chekiang region. In Yüeh, in ancient times, it was the custom to beat the drum and blow the flute to welcome spring.

Yün-chung, see Feng T'ang.

Finding List for Alternate Texts

Principal texts

NTECT   Wang Chung-wen, ed. *Nan T'ang erh chu tz'u.*
CST   T'ang Kuei-chang, ed. *Ch'üan Sung tz'u.*

Li Yü

   Alternate: Peng Ting-ch'iu, ed. *Ch'üan T'ang shih* (CTS). (All varia-
tions are also in NTECT footnotes.)

Ch'ing p'ing yüeh	NTECT 19* CTS 2162
Hsiang chien huan	NTECT 24* CTS 2162
Yü mei jen	NTECT 40* CTS 2163
Lang t'ao sha	NTECT 49* CTS 2163
Hsiang chien huan	NTECT 63* CTS 2162

Lin Pu

   Alternate: Hu Yün-i, ed. *Sung tz'u hsüan* (Hu).

Hsiang szu ling	CST 7* Hu p. 6

Chang Hsien

   Alternate: Chu Tsu-mou, compiler. *Sung tz'u san pai shou* (300).

P'u sa man	CST 85* 300 p. 7

Yen Shu

   Alternate: Chu Tsu-mou, compiler. *Sung tz'u san pai shou* (300).

Tieh lien hua	CST 109* 300 p. 16

The poem is sometimes attributed to Feng Yen-ssu.

Chang Shen

Alternate: Hu Yün-i, ed. *Sung tz'u hsüan* (Hu).

Li t'ing yen   CST 111* Hu p. 23

Ou-yang Hsiu

Alternate: Chu Tsu-mou, compiler. *Sung tz'u san pai shou* (300).

Ch'ing yü an   CST 161* 300 p. 25

Su Shih

Alternate: Su Shih. *Tung-p'o tzu* (TPT).

Nien nu chiao   CST 282* TPT #130
Nien nu chiao "Mid-Autumn"   CST 330* TPT #131
Wang chiang nan   CST 295* TPT #62
Pu suan tzu   CST 295* TPT #142
Chiang ch'eng tzu   CST 299* TPT #114

Chou Pang-yen

Alternates: Chu Tsu-mou, compiler. *Sung tz'u san pai shou* (300).
            Hu Yün-i, ed. *Sung tz'u hsüan* (Hu).

Man t'ing fang   CST 601* 300 p. 94
Kuo ch'in lou   CST 602* 300 p. 96
Chieh yü hua   CST 608* Hu p. 134
Liu ch'ou   CST 610* Hu p. 132

Li Ch'ing-chao

Alternate: Li Ch'ing-chao. *Nu tz'u jen Li Ch'ing-chao* (NTJ).

T'ien tzu ts'ai sang tzu   CST 930* NTJ p. 55
Lin chiang hsien   CST 929* NTJ p. 69
Ju meng ling   CST 935* NTJ p. 101

FINDING LIST FOR ALTERNATE TEXTS

Lu Yu

Alternate: Lu Yu. *Lu Yu hsüan chi* (Lu Yu).

Ch'üeh ch'iao hsien   CST 1595 * Lu Yu p. 197

Hsin Ch'i-chi

Alternates: Hsin Chi-chi. *Chia-hsüan tz'u* (CHT).
            Chu Tsu-mou, compiler. *Sung tz'u san pai shou* (300).

Shui lung yin   CST 1869 * 300 p. 157
Man chiang hung   CST 1870 * CHT p. 46
Nien nu chiao   CST 1874 * 300 p. 155
P'u sa man   CST 1880 * 300 p. 164
Mu lan hua man   CST 1881 * CHT p. 21
Chu ying t'ai chin   CST 1882 * CHT p. 80
Ho hsin lang   CST 1914 * 300 p. 153

Chiang K'uei

Alternate: Hu Yün-i, ed. *Sung tz'u hsüan* (Hu).

Ling lung szu fan   CST 2178 * Hu p. 352

About the Illustrations

*What is not used up in poetry overflows to become calligraphy
and is transformed to become painting.*   —SU SHIH

Most of the illustrations in this book are by poets, five by those whose work
is translated here—Li Yü, Su Shih, Chao Chi, and Lu Yu—eight by people
very like them, mostly of their circle, and a few by professional artists and
artisans of the time.

The calligraphy is mainly single characters or lines from longer works;
each detail is kinetic, individual, original—a self-contained image. None
has any semantic relevance to the poems in this book. Calligraphy as an art
form—often very difficult even for experts to read—is valued quite apart
from what it says.

Li Yü, Su Shih, and Chao Chi number among the great calligraphers of
all time, as do Huang T'ing-chien and Mi Fu, who were part of Su Shih's
circle, and Chao Meng-fu, a later disciple. Chao's "Orchids and Bamboo"
and the calligraphic, vibrant "Narcissi" by his cousin Chao Meng-chien—
twelve feet of them—epitomize the painting of the scholar-poets. Su
Shih's hanging scroll is one of many interpretations of bamboo by these—
they called themselves amateur—artists. As government officials they
identified with bamboo's resilience: it would bend but not break.

Many of the lyrical images in the work of professional painters come
from literature. The lone fisherman (Ma Yüan), the plum branch in the
moonlight (Yen Hui), the skiff in the wilderness (style of Hsia Kuei)—all
are familiar verbal images.

"The Phoenix," which may be even earlier than Sung dynasty, repre-
sents a mythical bird in whose pompadours and curls one recognizes the
"phoenix hair-style" so popular with the young women of the time.

Bush, *Early Chinese Texts on Painting*, p. 196

Credits

Frontispiece: Ma Yüan (active 1180–1230). "Ch'iu Chiang Yü Yin T'u." Ink on paper. Collection of the National Palace Museum. Taipei, Taiwan, Republic of China.

Mi Fu (1051–1107). Detail from a handscroll. "Sailing on the Wu River." Forty-four lines in semirunning and cursive script. Ink on paper. The Metropolitan Museum of Art, gift of John M. Crawford in honor of Professor Wen Fong (1984.174.(5)).

Li Yü (937–979). Detail from a facsimile, Shanghai, 1936. Courtesy Starr Library, Columbia University.

Chao Meng-chien (1199–1267?). "Narcissi." Section of a handscroll, detail. Ink on paper. The Metropolitan Museum of Art, gift of the Dillon Fund (1973.120.4).

Yen Hui (active from before 1279). "Plum Blossoms in Moonlight." Fan painting mounted as album leaf, 25.5 × 27.6 cm., ink on silk. Copyright the Cleveland Museum of Art. Andrew R. and Martha Holden Jenning Fund (78.49).

Huang T'ing-chien (1045–1105). Detail from a handscroll. "Biographies of Lien P'o and Lin Hsiang-ju." Abridged version of chapter 81 of the *Shih chi* of Ssu-ma Chien (145–before 86 B.C.). Two hundred and three lines in cursive script. Ink on paper. The Metropolitan Museum of Art, bequest of John M. Crawford (1989.363.4 section 15).

Mi Fu (1052–1107). Detail from a handscroll. "Sailing on the Wu River." Forty-four lines in semirunning and cursive script. Ink on paper. Metropolitan Museum of Art, gift of John M. Crawford in honor of Professor Wen Fong (1984.174.(6)).

254

Mi Fu (1052–1107). Single line, detail in *Yi-pi shu* from "Letter Written by Mi Fei (Mi Fu)." Collection of the National Palace Museum. Taipei, Taiwan, Republic of China.

Huang T'ing-chien (1045–1105). Detail from a handscroll. "Biographies of Lien P'o and Lin Hsiang-ju." Two hundred and three lines cursive script. Metropolitan Museum of Art, bequest of John M. Crawford (1989.363.4 section 13).

"Figure of Phoenix" (T'ang–Sung dynasties). Silver. Bequest of Charles B. Hoyt. Courtesy Museum of Fine Arts, Boston.

Su Shih (1037–1101). "Bamboo." Hanging scroll mounted as a handscroll. Ink on paper. The Metropolitan Museum of Art, bequest of John M. Crawford, Jr., 1988 (1989.363.3 section 1).

Su Shih (1037–1101). Single character detail from "Poem Written by Su Shih in Hsing-ts'ao Style." Ink on paper, 34 × 144.5 cm. Collection of the National Palace Museum. Taipei, Taiwan, Republic of China.

Ma Lin (ca. 1180–1256). "Orchids." Album leaf. Ink and light color on silk. The Metropolitan Museum of Art, gift of the Dillon Fund (1973.120.10).

Chao Chi (Emperor Sung Hui-tsung; 1082–1135). Single character detail. "Poem and Calligraphy by Sung Hui-tsung" ("slender gold style"). Ink on silk, 27 × 265.9 cm. Collection of the National Palace Museum. Taipei, Taiwan, Republic of China.

Chao Meng-fu (1254–1322). "Bamboo, Rocks, and Lonely Orchids." Handscroll, 50.5 × 144 cm. Ink on paper. Detail. Copyright the Cleveland Museum of Art, John L. Severance Fund (63.515).

255

.

Lu Yu (1125–1210). Detail from "A Letter Written by Lu Yu." Ink on paper. Collection of the National Palace Museum. Taipei, Taiwan, Republic of China.

Chao Meng-fu (1254–1322). Single character detail from a hanging scroll, "A Summer Idyll." Ink on silk. Metropolitan Museum of Art, bequest of John M. Crawford, Jr. (1989.363.31).

Style of Hsia Kuei (1180–1230). "River Landscape with Boatman," Ming dynasty (1368–1644). Ink on silk. The Metropolitan Museum of Art, Fletcher Fund, 1947. The A.W. Bahr Collection. (47.18.40).

·

ABOUT THE ILLUSTRATIONS

Bibliography

Baxter, Glen W. *Index to the Imperial Register of Tz'u Prosody (Chin-ting tz'u-pu)*. Harvard Yenching Institute Studies, 15. Cambridge: Harvard University Press, 1956.

——"Metrical Origins of the Tz'u." In John L. Bishop, ed., *Studies in Chinese Literature*. Cambridge: Harvard University Press, 1956.

Birch, Cyril, ed. *Studies in Chinese Literary Genres*. Berkeley: University of California Press, 1974.

Bryant, Daniel. *Lyric Poets of the Southern T'ang: Li Yü and Feng Yen-ssu*. Vancouver: University of British Columbia Press, 1982.

Bush, Susan and Hsio-yen Shih. *Early Chinese Texts on Painting*. Cambridge: Harvard University Press, 1985.

Chang, Kang-i Sun. *The Evolution of Chinese Tz'u Poetry: From Late T'ang to Northern Sung*. Princeton: Princeton University Press, 1980.

Chaves, Jonathan. "The Tz'u Poetry of Wen T'ing-yün." M.A. thesis. Columbia University, 1966.

Chen, Shih-chuan. "The Rise of Tz'u Reconsidered." *Journal of the American Oriental Society* (1970), 90(2):232–242.

Chu Tsu-mou, compiler. *Sung tz'u san pai shou*. Annotated by T'ang Kuei-chang. Hong Kong: Chung hua shu-chu, 1961.

Duke, Michael S. *Lu You*. Boston: Twayne, 1977.

Ebrey, Patricia Buckley, ed. *Chinese Civilization and Society: A Sourcebook*. New York: Free Press, 1981.

Egan, Ronald C. *The Literary Works of Ou-yang Hsiu (1007–72)*. Cambridge: Cambridge University Press, 1984.

Fong, Grace S. *Wu Wenying and the Art of Southern Song (Sung) Ci (Tz'u) Poetry*. New Haven: Yale University Press, 1976.

Fong, Wen C. *Beyond Representation: Chinese Painting and Calligraphy, Eighth–Fourteenth Century*. New York: Metropolitan Museum. New Haven: Yale University Press, 1992.

Franke, Herbert ed., *Sung Biographies*. Wiesbaden: Franz Steiner Verlag, 1976.

Frankel, Hans H. *The Flowering Plum and the Palace Lady: Interpretations of Chinese Poetry*. New Haven: Yale University Press, 1976.

Fusek, Lois, trans. *Among the Flowers: The Hua-chien chi*. New York: Columbia University Press, 1982.

Gernet, Jacques. *Daily Life in China on the Eve of the Mongol Invasion, 1250–1276*. Trans. H. M. Wright. Stanford: Stanford University Press, 1962.

Hightower, James Robert. "The Songs of Chou Pang-yen." *Harvard Journal of Asiatic Studies* (1977), 37:233–272.

——"The Songwriter Liu Yung." *Harvard Journal of Asiatic Studies* (1981), 41(2):323–376.

——"The Songwriter Liu Yung (II)." *Harvard Journal of Asiatic Studies* (1982), 42(1):5–66.

Hsin Ch'i-chi. *Chia-hsüan tz'u pien-nien ch'ien-chu*. Ed. Teng Kuang-ming. Shanghai: Ku tien wen hsüeh ch'u pan she, 1957.

Hu, P'in-ch'ing. *Li Ch'ing-chao*. New York: Twayne, 1966.

Hu, Yün-i ed. *Sung tz'u hsüan*. Hong Kong: Chung hua shu chu, 1970, 1977.

Kao, Yu-kung. "Chinese Lyric Aesthetics." In Alfreda Murck and Wen C. Fong, eds., *Words and Images: Chinese Poetry, Calligraphy and Painting*. Princeton: Princeton University Press, 1991.

Landau, Julie. "The Perfect Gentleman." *Encounter* (June 1988), 71(1):48–56.

Li Ch'ing-chao. *Nu tz'u jen Li Ch'ing-chao*. Ed. She Hsueh-man. Taipei: Wen Kuang t'u shu kung, 1961.

Lin, Shuen-fu. *The Transformation of the Chinese Lyrical Tradition: Chiang K'uei and Southern Sung Tz'u*. Princeton: Princeton University Press, 1978.

Liu Hsieh. *Wen hsin tiao lung. The Literary Mind and the Carving of the Dragons*. Bilingual. Trans. Vincent Yu-chung Shih. Hong Kong: Chinese University Press, 1983.

Liu, James J. Y. *The Art of Chinese Poetry*. Chicago: Chicago University Press, 1962.

——*Chinese Theories of Literature.* Chicago: University of Chicago Press, 1975.

——*Major Lyricists of the Northern Sung.* Princeton: Princeton University Press, 1974.

——"Some Literary Qualities of the Lyric (Tz'u)." In Cyril Birch, ed., *Studies in Chinese Literary Genres.* Berkeley: University of California Press, 1974.

Liu, James T. C. "An Early Sung Reformer: Fan Chung-yen." In John K. Fairbank, ed., *Chinese Thought and Institutions.* Chicago: University of Chicago Press, 1957.

——*Ou-yang Hsiu: An Eleventh-Century Neo-Confucianist.* Stanford: Stanford University Press, 1967.

——*Reform in Sung China: Wang An-shih (1021–1086) and His New Policies.* Cambridge: Harvard University Press, 1959.

Liu, Wu-chi and Irving Y. Lo, eds. *Sunflower Splendor: Three Thousand Years of Chinese Poetry.* New York: Anchor, 1975.

Lo, Irving Y. *Hsin Ch'i-chi.* New York: Twayne, 1971.

——"Thirty Lyrics by Hsin Ch'i-chi." *K'uei Hsing* (1971), 1:30–39. Bloomington: Indiana University Press.

Lu Yu. *Lu Yu hsüan chi.* Ed. Chu Tung-jun. Shanghai, 1962.

Mather, Richard B., trans. *Shih-shuo Hsin-yü: A New Account of Tales of the World by Liu I-ch'ing.* Minneapolis: University of Minnesota Press, 1976.

Murck, Alfreda and Wen C. Fong, eds. *Words and Images: Chinese Poetry, Calligraphy, and Painting.* Princeton: Princeton University Press, 1991.

Owen, Stephen. *Remembrances: The Experience of the Past in Classical Chinese Literature.* Cambridge: Harvard University Press, 1986.

P'eng Ting-ch'iu et al., eds. *Ch'üan T'ang shih.* Shanghai: Shanghai ku chi ch'u pan she, 1986.

Rickett, Adele Austin, ed. *Chinese Approaches to Literature from Confucius to Liang Ch'i-chao.* Princeton: Princeton University Press, 1955.

Rickett, Adele Austin. *Wang Kuo-wei's Jen-chien Tz'u Hua: A Study in Chinese Literary Criticism.* Hong Kong: Hong Kong University Press, 1977.

Shih, Vincent Yu-chung, trans. *The Literary Mind and the Carving of the Dragons: A Study of Thought Patterns in Chinese Literature.* Hong Kong: Chinese University Press, 1983.

Siren, Osvald. *The Chinese on the Art of Painting: Translations and Comments.* New York: Schocken, 1963.

Soong, Stephen C., ed. *Song Without Music: Chinese Tz'u Poetry.* Hong Kong: Chinese University Press, 1980.

Su Shih. *Tung p'o tz'u.* Ed. Ts'ao Shu-ming. Hong Kong: Universal Book, 1968.

T'ang Kuei-chang, ed. *Ch'üan Sung tz'u.* 5 vols. Peking: Chung hua shu-chu, 1965.

Wagner, Marsha L. *The Lotus Boat: The Origins of Tz'u in T'ang Popular Culture.* New York: Columbia University Press, 1984.

Wang Chung-wen, ed. *Nan T'ang erh-chu tz'u chiao-ting.* Peking: Jen-ming wen-hsueh ch'u pan she, 1957.

Watson, Burton. *Chinese Lyricism: Shih Poetry from the Second to the Twelfth Century.* New York: Columbia University Press, 1971.

Watson, Burton, trans. and ed. *The Columbia Book of Chinese Poetry: From Early Times to the Thirteenth Century.* New York: Columbia University Press, 1984.

Watson, Burton, trans. *The Old Man Who Does as He Pleases: Poems and Prose by Lu Yu.* New York: Columbia University Press, 1973.

——*Records of the Grand Historian of China Translated from the Shih chi of Ssu-ma Ch'ien.* New York: Columbia University Press, 1961.

——*Su Tung-p'o: Selections from a Sung Dynasty Poet.* New York: Columbia University Press, 1965.

Wixted, John Timothy. *The Song Poetry of Wei Chuang (836–910).* Tempe: Center for Asian Studies, Arizona State University, 1979.

——*Poems on Poetry: Literary Criticism by Yuan Hao-wen (1190–1257).* Wiesbaden: Franz Steiner Verlag, 1982.

Yates, Robin D. S. *Washing Silk: The Life and Selected Poetry of Wei Chuang (834?–910).* Cambridge: Harvard University Press, 1988.

Yip, Wai-lim. *Chinese Poetry: Major Modes and Genres.* Berkeley: University of California Press, 1976.

Yoshikawa, Kojiro. *An Introduction to Sung Poetry.* Trans. Burton Watson. Cambridge: Harvard University Press, 1967.

Yu, Pauline. *The Reading of Imagery in the Chinese Poetic Tradition.* Princeton: Princeton University Press, 1987.

Index to Tune Titles

INDEX TO TUNE TITLES

Index

267

Other Works in the Columbia Asian Studies Series

Translations from the Asian Classics

OTHER WORKS IN THE ASIAN STUDIES SERIES

Studies in Asian Culture

OTHER WORKS IN THE ASIAN STUDIES SERIES

Companions to Asian Studies

Approaches to the Oriental Classics, ed. Wm. Theodore de Bary	1959
Early Chinese Literature, by Burton Watson. Also in paperback ed.	1962
Approaches to Asian Civilizations, ed. Wm. Theodore de Bary and Ainslie T. Embree	1964
The Classic Chinese Novel: A Critical Introduction, by C. T. Hsia. Also in paperback ed.	1968
Chinese Lyricism: Shih Poetry from the Second to the Twelfth Century, tr. Burton Watson. Also in paperback ed.	1971
A Syllabus of Indian Civilization, by Leonard A. Gordon and Barbara Stoler Miller	1971
Twentieth-Century Chinese Stories, ed. C. T. Hsia and Joseph S. M. Lau. Also in paperback ed.	1971
A Syllabus of Chinese Civilization, by J. Mason Gentzler, 2d ed.	1972
A Syllabus of Japanese Civilization, by H. Paul Varley, 2d ed.	1972
An Introduction to Chinese Civilization, ed. John Meskill, with the assistance of J. Mason Gentzler	1973
An Introduction to Japanese Civilization, ed. Arthur E. Tiedemann	1974
Ukifune: Love in the Tale of Genji, ed. Andrew Pekarik	1982
The Pleasures of Japanese Literature, by Donald Keene	1988
A Guide to Oriental Classics, ed. Wm. Theodore de Bary and Ainslie T. Embree; third edition ed. Amy Vladek Heinrich, 2 vols.	1989

Introduction to Asian Civilizations

Wm. Theodore de Bary, Editor
Sources of Japanese Tradition, 1958; paperback ed., 2 vols., 1964
Sources of Indian Tradition, 1958; paperback ed., 2 vols., 1964; 2d ed., 1988
Sources of Indian Tradition, 1988; 2d ed., 2 vols.
Sources of Chinese Tradition, 1960; paperback ed., 2. vols., 1964

Neo-Confucian Studies

OTHER WORKS IN THE ASIAN STUDIES SERIES

Modern Asian Literature Series

OTHER WORKS IN THE ASIAN STUDIES SERIES

Designer: Teresa Bonner
Text: Goudy Old Style
Compositor: The Composing Room of Michigan
Printer: Edwards Brothers
Binder: Edwards Brothers